PRAISE FOR *SINGLE BUT DATING*

Single But Dating is the perfect book for any woman seeking mindful guidance on her romantic journey.

Dr. Nikki is like a wise big sister who will hold your hand through the dating process and encourage you to be unapologetic about what you desire in your relationships. Learn to awaken your authentic self and build the best love life for you.

This book will help you date with confidence and have a lot of fun along the way!—Gabrielle Bernstein, #1 New York Times Bestselling author of *The Universe Has Your Back*

In a technologically-advanced day and age where every blip and beep on our phones and laptops impacts the way women view themselves, *Single But Dating* offers a well-informed look on staying self-confident, self-aware and empowered to love ourselves, while we look for romantic love with someone else.—Jenny Gaither and Charina Lumley, Founder and COO of Movemeant Foundation (www.movemeant.org)

Love is vital in our lives and has powerful effects in our brains. Dr. Nikki offers a fresh perspective to help women find this precious gift in our changing world.—Dr. Mike Dow, NY Times bestselling author of *The Brain Fog Fix*

Dr. Nikki not only shares incredibly helpful and insightful information on how to navigate dating and enjoying single life in our modern world, she also candidly reveals personal experiences that all readers can relate to. *Single But Dating* is sure to inspire readers. —Sunny Rodgers, Playboy Radio Host

Modern dating is constantly changing. In *Single But Dating* Dr. Nikki Goldstein establishes and embraces a new relationship status for women. The book is a celebration of single life, and a rejection of the pressures which society has placed on women in the past.—Charly Lester, Founder of The Dating Awards & Dating Expert Academy

Dr. Nikki Goldstein tells it like it is in *Single But Dating!* Thank goodness there is a dating book for the modern woman who wants to enjoy her life while single and dating, not hurry it up to get down the aisle. We love Dr. Nikki's useful tips to milk every ounce of fun and knowledge out of this period in life.—Ellen Fein and Sherrie Schneider, Authors of *The Rules* and *Not Your Mother's Rules*

Dr. Nikki Goldstein takes a refreshing look at dating and is reframing "happily ever after" for modern daters. If you're looking for practical advice to ensure that you relish in the journey that is dating, be sure to check out *Single But Dating.*—Jessica O'Reilly, Author of *The New Sex Bible*

Dr. Nikki's book is fun sexy and smart. I love that she shares intimate details about her egg freezing experience. *Single But Dating* is the new dating rule book for today's woman.—Dr. Aimee Eyvazzadeh, Fertility Specialist

Far from being sad and lonely, being single can be one of the most exciting, formative times of your life. *Single But Dating* shows women how to enjoy dating in a modern world and make the most out of those gloriously free experimental years.—Tracey Cox, Author and International Sex and Relationship Expert

Dr. Nikki gives perfect advice for the millennial woman trying to make it in the dating world. And even though I've never been one for homework, the exercises included are good for everything from helping you hone down what you're really looking for in a relationship to celebrating being single. Plus, she even gives advice on how to send a sexy pic, which I *really* appreciate in a book. *Single but Dating* is fun, practical, and a must read. I loved it!!—Writer Alison Segel

Single But Dating

A Field Guide to Dating in the Digital Age

DR. NIKKI GOLDSTEIN

NOTHING BUT THE TRUTH, LLC

SAN FRANCISCO

Published in 2017 by Nothing But The Truth, LLC
NothingButtheTruth.com
Nothing But The Truth name and logo are trademarks of Nothing
But The Truth Publishing, LLC.

LIBRARY OF CONGRESS CATALOGING-IN-PUBLICATION DATA

Goldstein, Dr. Nikki
Single but Dating:
A Field Guide to Dating in the Digital Age
Mickey Nelson, Editor.

Library of Congress Control Number: 2017905322

ISBN: 978-0-9972962-5-9 (Paperback)
ISBN: 978-0-9972962-6-6 (E-book)

Printed in the United States of America
2017

*Pseudonyms have been used in this book and other details altered where
necessary to protect the identity and privacy of people mentioned.*

*Every effort has been made to acknowledge and contact the copyright
holders for permission to reproduce material contained in this book. Any
copyright holders who have been inadvertently omitted from acknowl-
edgments and credits should contact the publisher, and omissions will be
rectified in subsequent editions.*

To my parents,
for teaching me how to love by loving me unconditionally

Dr. Nikki Goldstein is Australia's modern-day expert on all things relating to sex and relationships. She has a unique ability to normalize the subjects of sex and relationships, and her fresh, balanced and candid views make her instantly relatable and approachable.

She holds a bachelor's degree in psychology, a postgraduate diploma in counseling and a doctorate in human sexuality; she is a highly credible authority on the topics of love, sex, dating, romance and relationships. Coming from a background as a family mediator who assisted in the process of divorce, she has an understanding of what makes and breaks relationships. She appears across many media avenues, such as TV, radio, podcasts and magazines, both in the US and Australia.

Twice voted Australia's Best Sex Educator, she's young, bright and honest and has lived many years of her life as a Single but Dating (SBD) woman.

Contents

Introduction

Being single used to mean that nobody wanted you. Now it
means you're pretty sexy and you're taking your time deciding
how you want your life to be and who you want to spend it with.
—Carrie Bradshaw, *Sex and the City*

The past can mold who we are and how we see the world. This
can become a block to many people moving forward, but it's
important to see your past as a step toward your future self. My
exploration of the Single but Dating (SBD) world came from
one of the most difficult times in my own life. I hope that this
book can also help you transform your SBD years into a time
of self-growth, self-exploration and increased self-esteem—all
while having a damn good time.

At the age of 22, I thought I had what I wanted. I had moved
in with my high school sweetheart, who, on paper, was everything I thought I should want. But cracks started to appear, and
I eventually woke up one day unable to stop crying, sleep, eat
or see a positive future for myself. It was one of the darkest
periods of my life and I eventually hit rock bottom. I thought
what I had was perfect, but in reality, I'd been blocking out
things I didn't want to see. It took me a long time to get clarity
on what I really wanted and needed.

During this time, I was diagnosed with a depressive episode,
which was the serious, scary and swift kick in the butt I needed
to address the issues I had been sugarcoating and ignoring. I

was in a job I didn't enjoy, a living situation that wasn't what I wanted and a relationship where I felt trapped. I didn't know what I wanted to change, just that my current situation was not making me happy and change was the only option. This high school sweetheart was the only man I had been with romantically and sexually, and staying in the relationship felt safe and familiar. In retrospect, I don't think I understood what a healthy relationship should feel like. I thought the difficulties I was experiencing were just part of loving someone, because at that point, I didn't know anything different.

This is the problem with falling in love young and it is also the reason why comparison and experience can be such important tools in working out what is right and wrong for you. Once we have more experiences in life and love, we can more fully understand what we want and need from our lives and love relationships.

Some people genuinely do fall in love young and want no one else. However, others (like me) merely think they are in love but deep down are unsure, having had little experience with this feeling before, trying to convince themselves that whatever they feel is how love is supposed to be. My mother used to tell me that she wished I'd had other partners before I met my boyfriend so I had something to compare my relationship to.

I had never imagined a life without this person and breaking up with him was sad and terrifying—one of the hardest decisions of my life. But it was a decision that deep down I knew I had to make. As it turns out, it was also one of my best decisions and the beginning of a life I had only dreamt of—and the birth of the idea of Single but Dating!

During the next period of my life, I wasn't exactly single—I didn't have lonely nights at home in my sweatpants—but I also wasn't in a committed relationship. I wanted a new term for this period in my life and Single but Dating was it! Now I want to help other women enjoy this period of time as much as I did.

I continued on a path that can only be described as self-discovery experimentation (*sexperimentation* and *sexploration*) and a bloody good time. I've always been the type of girl who wants to try everything in life, and for the first time as a Single but Dating (SBD) woman, I experienced what it truly meant to be free.

Discovering what I really wanted wasn't easy. I quit my job as a family mediator, moved into my bachelorette pad and started studying for a doctorate in human sexuality, a degree in which you are encouraged to experience the breadth of human sexuality firsthand. Over the course of this research, everything I'd ever thought was normal or expected of me sexually and romantically was questioned and challenged. I began to feel like I'd previously been stuck in a tug-of-war between what I thought was right and what I really wanted.

As the years went on, I slowly started to work out the type of men whose company I enjoyed, what I liked and didn't like about dating, the varying outcomes of different dating and sexual scenarios, and what different levels of happiness and passion with another human being felt like.

No one teaches you how to date (although I wish they would). In these SBD years, I taught myself—albeit the hard way—dating and the consequences involved (including judgment from other women). Challenging established ideas and preconceived notions about love and sex made me realize I had choices in the way I wanted to live and the power to enact those choices.

There was no name for the life I was living. People would often ask if I was seeing someone and I would look at them confused, wondering at all the possible answers I could give them. I might have been on a few dates that week, hooked up with a friend or just started seeing someone, but I wasn't in what I would call a relationship by traditional standards. I also wasn't at home eating ice cream and waiting for the phone to ring, and I absolutely hated using the word *single*!

The word *single* still seems to elicit a certain level of pity or shame. Why must it be immediately followed by the suggestion of a setup? I desperately wanted to reassure people that there was no lack of men in my life and that I was in fact choosing to explore my options, but I was scared of being judged for the life I was living or labeled with negative terms like *promiscuous* or *slutty*.

I didn't feel that there was enough outside validation of the choice to explore my sexuality. I did feel some support, but I also felt I could be rebuked quickly if I crossed someone's invisible line of propriety. I had to find validation from within myself.

As I gave myself the freedom to enjoy my SBD years and learned to follow my inner voice, I began to create a life I truly wanted, regardless of the *shoulds* and *should nots* in the world around me. At some stage, I did decide once again that I wanted children and marriage, but this time, I came to that decision out of choice, not out of obligation. (I always did warn my parents I would do things my way!)

I wanted to know from experience that what was in front of me was right for me, not be left questioning what else out there may be better. I now know what it's like to be with someone when it just works and I know that because I'm able to compare it with times when things didn't work.

What Is Single but Dating?

Looking at my Facebook page one day, I saw the options for my relationship status: Single, In a Relationship, Married or It's Complicated. I suddenly remembered all the forms I'd ever been asked to fill out and the options for my relationship status: single, married, widowed or divorced. If you are friends with someone and exploring the idea of entering a relationship, or casually hooking up with them without the intention to make it official, or even just dating someone but not in a serious relationship or married to them, you are forced to declare that you are single, a word that is loaded with connotations. A Single but Dating (SBD) woman is not entirely single, not entirely *not* single, but somewhere in between while she tries to work out what she wants from her love, sex and dating lives. You may be just out of a relationship or happily single and wanting to live your SBD years even better. You may have been Single but Dating for a while but not enjoying it fully. However you got here, my hope is to give you some guidance and validation to help you build the best love life for you.

Despite the fact that women are waiting longer and longer to get married or choosing not to get married at all, society has yet to validate how SBD women go about their romantic and sexual lives, and that takes away some of our ability to really enjoy these important years.

We are dating differently, loving differently and having sex differently, and it's up to us to make that journey enjoyable. Marrying a perfect-on-paper guy is no longer the ultimate goal to love and life. We don't need to change ourselves to fit into the ideal standards for men. We need support, encouragement, empowerment and information in order to get the most out of the rapidly changing dating environment, and this book is here to give you that. We need to be the best version of ourselves, so that we are able to date from an authentic and healthy state of mind—free from the *shoulds* and *what-ifs* that often plague our brains and steal our joy.

SBD women are living the lives that men have been able to for years, and sexuality is a big part of this. In the past, women exploring their bodies and what to do with them was only accepted inside the bounds of a relationship (and unfortunately, there are still some people who hold this view). I will give you plenty of tools so that you can pave your individual path to loving the sex and dating life you have no matter what other people think.

Part of this SBD life is experimenting with sexual urges. This is a time for you to sexplore, sexperiment and discover what you want. Some people stay in the SBD lifestyle longer than others, some people come in and out, and others live the SBD life continually. Whatever you choose, one thing is clear: dating has changed for women. It's no longer about settling down and finding someone to take care of us; rather, it's about discovering what we want, what type of relationship we want to be in, making no apologies for it and creating our best reality.

SBD women are just modern women in a complex dating world, with more choices in love and life and a less immediate need to settle.

Mindful Dating

*The question is how would your life be transformed if you
chose to love this time for once with all your intelligence?*
—Cheryl Strayed

Too many times very early in the process of getting to know someone, I would start to consider crazy and impossible-to-tell things like whether a person was right to be in an official relationship with, whether I saw a future with them, if I could marry them or have children with them, what my parents would think and so on. I didn't end up enjoying their company and I wasn't even able to get to know them because I was too busy imagining the hypothetical future.

If you are like me, then this is a habit that you need to break ASAP. Learning how to just date a guy without wondering from the get-go about a future with them is key to enjoying dates and seeing and getting to know the person in front of you. A theoretical or fantastical thought process stops us from being present. The present can actually be really pleasant if you give it a chance. We live in a society that is increasingly focused on mindfulness— we are taught to be present in yoga class, on our stationary bikes and when we are eating our food, so why shouldn't we be incorporating this mentality into our dating lives?

Mindfulness is when you focus on what is happening around you *right now*—your sensations and feelings—without judging yourself or others. It makes perfect sense to take a similar approach with the men in our lives and it's a good reason to practice meditation regularly as an SBD woman. By dating mindfully, you may be more dismissive of superficial qualities and stop missing out on great guys because you are not fully in the present moment.

In a world where we are stressed, anxious, overworked and bombarded by external influences, it can be good to stop and do something that slows your mind down: yoga, meditation or just sitting still—anything that allows you to stop and calmly process what's going on inside. I find that guided meditation from apps and free playlists helps me to slow down for 10 minutes a day and focus on breathing, giving me a clear mind to face any obstacles or stressors. As an added benefit, these practices help me get to know myself better. How will you work out what factors are affecting you and what you can do about it them you don't have the time to make sense of them?

We can get depressed when we think about the past, which we can't change, and we get worried when we think about the future, which is something we can't predict.

> *If you are depressed you are living in the past.*
> *If you are anxious you are living in the future.*
> *If you are at peace you are living in the present.*
> —Lao Tzu

When we get depressed or anxious, these feelings can cloud our judgment and spoil positive emotions we are experiencing. Dating these days can sometimes feel like a race against time, but if you do want to date to have a long-term partner and family, it's important to slow down and look at the scenario and the men in front of you with a clear and present mind, free of past triggers or future fears.

An Activity from Wellness Coach and Founder of *Stars Like You*, Damian Rocks:

A great technique to use when you are meeting new people or encounter a stressful situation is to imagine yourself surrounded by a bubble of light. This works as powerful visualization for creating the environment that you want and sets a tone that others respond to. It's not so much that you are actually creating a ball of light around yourself; rather, it sets an intention that will affect the unconscious space connecting you with others. Best of all, you can choose the color to suit the situation, and reflect what you need in the moment.

For example, a ball of pink light reinforces the idea that you are open to loving encounters and only good things can come your way. This can help if you tend to have problems with intimacy.

A ball of blue light will work to create distance between you and those in your environment, so you can separate your own feelings from what you may pick up from the people around you. This is great if you "pick up" the energy of other people too much.

For a totally different effect, imagining yourself surrounded by mirrors will deflect any negative energy that might be coming your way and return it to its source of origin. If you're stuck on a bad date with someone who is draining your energy, then putting up a mirror will create a demarcation zone that can give you breathing space to manage your exit.

I'm Single. So Sue Me!

Being single is a part of everyone's journey at some point and it is a shame that we aren't taught how to really enjoy those stretches of our lives. There are 126 million single people in the US, and the average age at which women marry recently jumped by five years after remaining unchanged for over a century. A 2013 study from the National Center for Family & Marriage Research found that the marriage rate was the lowest it had been in over a century. Women are living the SBD stretches of life for longer than ever before, but we aren't given enough tools or support to help us successfully navigate these periods. There are tons of books about how to land a guy and books about why statistics are not in your favor to do so, but there isn't enough talk about how fun and empowering this time in your life can be!

There is still a certain amount of societal validation that comes from being in a relationship, with many choosing to flaunt their relationship status to the world either in person or on social media (we all have at least one of those chicks in our feed). Sometimes there is a fine line between being proud of someone who is in your life and using the presence of a partner to elevate our self-worth and self-esteem. I once heard of a woman Photoshopping her boyfriend into her social media posts even after they'd broken up, because she felt too ashamed to be pictured alone. What a horrible feeling and a colossal waste of her precious time.

I'm good enough for someone else to love and choose me. The pursuit of this type of validation can lead women into relationships with the simple agenda of making themselves feel good, even if that means picking a partner who isn't a great fit or who doesn't treat them well. As an SBD woman, there may not always be someone to validate you. That is why building self-esteem is so crucial: you have to love the person you are enough so that another person's desires are just an added bonus. Healthy self-esteem is integral to a healthy life and healthy love.

There is absolutely nothing wrong with being single and there is nothing wrong with you if you are; that's why you can now add "but dating" to that word. As you read on, you'll have a lot more tools to help you enjoy and appreciate this time in your life.

Celebrating Single

We are living at a time when the number of single people is now greater than those who are married, and it's not for a lack of men. Women once had to marry for financial security and in order to have a family, which is no longer the case. Marriage is no longer an obligation but a choice, as it should be. I for one would always prefer to be single than in the wrong relationship!

As lovely as it can be to be with someone and in love, we also need to stop and celebrate the fact that women these days can be single by choice and that this single life is not a negative at all, but a beautiful thing. We don't hear that message enough! The truth is that most of the single women and men roaming this earth are in fact not entirely single. They date and they have sex. We need to give more acceptance to this in-between status and not only embrace the fact that we can now live it but also recognize how amazing it can be! It's important to explore how to date, have sex and possibly even get into a relationship while not shaming the status of single, but celebrating it.

Exercise—Celebrating Single

It's one thing for me to tell you how amazing single life can be, but it's important for you to highlight some of the things you can do in your current relationship status that you might not be able to do when with a partner. Below, write down three things that will help you celebrate being single (or single but dating). Mine are taking up the entire bed, having my bathroom covered in makeup and hair accessories and doing what I want to do when I want to do it.

1. _____

_____

_____

2. _____

_____

_____

3. _____

_____

_____

Finding Love, the SBD Way

The SBD life may be about having fun, dating lots of men and enjoying all the experiences between the sheets, but it's also a life that can be used to find real love if that's what you want. Often when women think about the future as they are dating, they are too focused on the factors they think matter— looks, security, whether their date is from a nice family, etc. Relationships in this state of being are about conforming to a list of categories, and people who manage this kind of relationship are often in denial or convincing themselves that what they have is real love. That isn't enough for everyone and it certainly wasn't enough for me.

In order to find passionate, can't-live-without-you love, you need to know what it is that makes you happy, the difference between healthy love and toxic emotions, and which situations and men are right for you and which are wrong, as well as let go of some of the programming you learned about what a relationship and a partner *should* look like for you.

Even if a long-term relationship is not your ultimate goal and you wish to remain in the SBD life continually, the longer you remain there, the more content your dating choices will make you as you better understand which dates to accept and which to reject.

My aim is not to change you by giving you the Single but Dating label, but rather to empower you to really enjoy the stage you're in. It's good to be free and it's good to explore and it's also good to know and understand potential outcomes and consequences of your choices in love and sex. This is the book I wish I could have read when I started this journey.

I have written this book from the viewpoint of an open-minded heterosexual female who predominantly dates men, as this is largely based on my personal experience (mixed with my professional knowledge) and because this is how I personally identify. That's not to say that a lot of the guidance, concepts and themes within these pages could not apply to or be used to success by those dating differently than me.

I also believe in the power of written words and that when we make declarations and statements on paper it further cements our ideas, intentions and goals. There are a series of written activities throughout this book to help challenge you and assist you in discovering things that you want.

Exercise—Goal Setting

The first activity I want you to do is write down the goals for your SBD journey. You can choose as many as you want, but it's important to have some direction. Your goal could be as simple as to have fun. It's still a direction. Looking back, my goal was to be truly and authentically happy and I can proudly say I've now achieved that. Maybe you want to pick better men or know yourself better, or maybe you just want to have more sex or better sex. Whatever pops into your head, don't judge it; write it down.

_____

_____

_____

_____

_____

_____

_____

_____

_____

_____

_____

_____

_____

_____

_____

_____

_____

Chapter 1

"I've a Feeling We're Not in Kansas Anymore"

We are becoming the men we wanted to marry.
—Gloria Steinem

Thanks to the modern and technology-driven environment we live in, dating has changed considerably. It's important to understand what some of these major changes are and how they impact you and your dating capabilities and options.

The *Should* Curse

We are brought up to believe we need to find a partner who ticks all the right boxes, because that's what we *should* do; date them for a while, because that's what we *should* do; move in with them after a while because that's what we *should* do; get engaged and married at a certain point in our life because that's what we *should* do; and then have children because that's what married couples *should* do. We are given the outline for a path that is supposed to ensure happiness, but this path really hasn't proven to be effective. Moreover, following a path laid down by tradition or religion for the masses doesn't allow you to find out what really works and doesn't work for you as an individual. As much as I consider myself a traditional woman at times and believe that the symbolism behind some traditions can be a peaceful influence in our lives, many traditional ideas are blindly accepted without questioning or reason, and this is not helpful to anyone.

We think we want certain things, but how often is that because we have been encouraged or programmed to want them? It's often difficult to tell the difference, as these learned wants sometimes feel like natural choices. I am going to push you to recognize some of the programming you might be carrying around from your culture, family, friends and upbringing, as it can block you from tapping into your truest, deepest self.

Because of these learned ideals, we may find ourselves dating men we think are the types of guys we *should* be dating. We date them in ways we think a woman *should* date and sleep with them when we think we *should*. We often don't challenge these ideas to make sure they reflect what *we really want*. These ideas can be planted in our heads at times and from people we don't even recall! The first step in dumping this old garbage out of your head is to be aware when it pops up.

It's Your Party and You Can Do What You Want To

*I love being single. I can come and go as I please
and stay out as late as I want to.*
—Eric Dickerson

Do things your way, not the way other people expect you to. When you try to force happiness, rationalizing it as "I'm doing what I *should* be doing, so I'm happy," you risk creating a type of happiness that won't last—or, worse, unhappiness that you won't admit. A lifestyle you don't proactively choose yourself but merely accept because it's expected will rarely be fulfilling.

As a modern SBD woman, it is vital that you challenge these *should* ideals. Challenging the *should* curse takes confidence: to step outside the boundaries of so-called normality, to bravely go against tradition and to explore what it is you want out of love, life, dating and sex. Being an SBD woman is not necessarily about breaking every tradition, but rather having the confidence to challenge those traditions, test uncharted waters and find the life that works for you, making sure you have fun, enjoy your experiences and learn from them along the way.

One of the biggest drawbacks to successful and fun dating can be the overwhelming number of options we have today. How do we know if we want certain things in love, life and dating unless we have tried them all or at least sampled enough?

In some cultures in the past (and in many areas, still), women—often at young ages—are forced against their will to marry partners they don't choose. Instead of education or careers, these young women must dedicate their lives to looking after a husband and children without question. No dating, no rights, no chance of finding passionate love and no opportunity for change. Although they can seem overwhelming, remember to be grateful for your options—not everyone has them. This will help you keep a positive mindset.

Trends Are Not Your Friends

We must be willing to get rid of the life we've planned,
so as to have the life that is waiting for us.
—Joseph Campbell

Sometimes *shoulds* arise because of a current trend. It's a natural human instinct to want to fit in, so if the masses are doing something, you may feel the need to follow suit.

Following the majority or "trend" is easy, and more in your face than ever before thanks to the omnipresence of social media. But while being validated by the masses may give us a feeling of belonging, it won't last, because if you aren't being true to you, you will eventually feel empty or lost and like something is missing.

We sometimes see a trend, something supported by many, as the reason we *should*. Dating multiple people at one time has arisen as a trend, as has "casual dating" (e.g., meeting for coffee or a drink rather than a dinner date). Has the way you've been dating been influenced by the masses around you, or is it something you have proactively chosen to do because it is best for you as an individual?

Exercise—Challenging the *Shoulds*

To help you challenge some of the *shoulds* that might be present in your life, I want you to write down five *shoulds* or *should nots* of dating that you live your life by. Next to each one, write where it came from. Did it come from yourself? From friends?

Maybe your family says you *should not* date outside of your religion? Society? Media? Social media? Because of a trend? If the response is anything other than self, challenge why you hold that belief in your life, how it serves you and if you want to keep it. Two examples from my life:

1. You *should not* sleep with a guy until five dates—my friend
2. You *should not* move in with a guy unless you are engaged—my family

Should or Should Not	Where It Came From
1. _____	_____
2. _____	_____
3. _____	_____
4. _____	_____
5. _____	_____

Behold: The Modern Female

Women who seek to be equal with men lack ambition.
—Marilyn Monroe

There is so much pressure on women these days to "have it all" and achieve equivalence to the alpha male. This brings challenges for dating. While the empowered attitude of the modern woman is worshipped by some men, it can cause dating drama and intimidation for others.

Women won the right to own vibrators and date multiple people while breaking the ceiling in the professional world, but we forgot to tell the men out there that an alpha female takes nothing away from what makes a man a man. We also forgot to make it clear that an alpha female can also be feminine and vulnerable. Some women think that being a modern woman means always being strong, hiding weakness or putting up a guard, but the truth is that there can be strength in being vulnerable enough to be open, confide in someone, ask for help or truly need something from the opposite sex. Everyone likes to feel needed, and for many men, feeling needed reassures them that they are the masculine element in the feminine/masculine equation. You can be a strong, empowered alpha female and still show vulnerability.

Vulnerability is letting down your walls enough to be open, let someone in and allow them to really get to know you. Being submissive is very different: it is being controlled. Being a smart woman means not only knowing how to be strong, but knowing how to be strong *and* vulnerable. It's not about competing with men but competing alongside them and knowing when to be strong enough to let go and sometimes let someone else take the lead or ask them for help.

SBD or Not Worthy?

Many women hide out in the SBD world, having sex with some men and dating others not because they want to experiment, but because they feel this lifestyle is their only option. They don't see the potential to make SBD scenarios into future relationships—they just have casual sex and date randomly because they don't feel worthy of love. This belief—which often stems from the fact that they don't have the confidence to love themselves—is what makes them appear off the market, convincing themselves and the men in their lives that casual hookups and flings are all they want. Their actions and behaviors signal that they are only available for casual dating, but their hearts and minds are saying, "I'm here because no one will commit to me, so this is all I can get."

For some, it takes strength to step out and live an SBD life, but for others, their lack of strength appears to be why they are here. They might not be really living the SBD life but are using the ostensible desire for a more casual dating lifestyle as a guise to hide insecurity. If you are hiding in the SBD lifestyle or using it as your excuse, then your first step is finding love for yourself from within yourself and caring for your self-worth.

Lose the Labels

> *By all means let's be open-minded, but not so*
> *open-minded that our brains drop out.*
> —Richard Dawkins

We tend to want to make sense of men we date: understand their thinking, put them into a *Mr. Right* or *Mr. Right Now* category, work out our place in their world and predict how it will all play out. But, just as we need to take a more liberal and flexible stance with our own labels, we also need to be more flexible when labeling others.

Categorizing and labeling can really impact how we see those we date, so at the very least, consider all men with a somewhat open mind. I say "somewhat" because having a fully open mind has landed me in lots of trouble and seen me date many men who are completely wrong! I've dated men with emotional baggage, with criminal pasts and questionable professional engagements, all in the name of being "open minded." (I'm probably too free-spirited for my own good, so please note that you don't have to be as open-minded as I have been.)

But one coffee or one drink and a little banter can't hurt. With luck, after giving a man some of your time and allowing yourself to see the person in front of you, you will be able to at least work out if he is interesting enough to want to see again. Don't let past perceptions or other people determine your future opinions, set categories or make rules that close your mind. The key is to focus on one thing that intrigues, interests or attracts you to another person and go with the flow, not worrying about what a person might be lacking from your dating wish list.

Careful What You Wish For

Charming villains have always had a decided social advantage over well-meaning people who chew with their mouths open.
—Judith Martin

You need to challenge your dating criteria, which often include general labels and categories: healthy, sense of humor, good-looking, corporate job, close family, a certain religion, a certain eye and hair color, penis size, circumcised, uncircumcised—and so on. I once had a friend who told me she would only date men who are circumcised. I would hate to know what would happen if she fell in love with someone who wasn't and how many amazing men she has let pass her by because of a little foreskin. You need to find the middle ground between being open-minded and standing firm on your deal-breakers, but you also need to examine why they are deal-breakers in the first place.

Should a date's low salary be the deal-breaker or him not treating you with kindness and respect? Aim for morals and values that are important to you, rather than a list of superficial attributes that could come and go. This is the difference between superficial and mature dating.

This is, of course, easier said than done. Many women are looking for security and love nice things. If economic security is what you want, understand why you want it and whether there are any consequences for wanting it. When we choose dates and hook up with people after making informed decisions—having thought about the reasons and influences behind our choices as well as the possible consequences—we are using the best mechanism we have to make the best decisions for an uncertain future.

People often pick partners based on qualities influenced by family, religion or social upbringing: the *shoulds*.

Religion is a big one. Being a Jewish woman, I see it a lot. I was not brought up very religious, so my parents only suggested another Jewish person might be best for me—they never forced me. My mother always reassured me that she wanted me to be happy above all else and that people love whom they love. For many people, however, dating outside of their faith is strictly out of bounds and it dictates their choices in dating and sex. Be aware if there is pressure from your family to date around religion or if being with someone of the same faith is also on your own dating wish list. If this is of utmost importance to you (and no one else), then I would advise you to not date anyone outside of your religion, as what will you do if you fall for them?

In addition to being aware of your own deal-breakers, you should be aware of any deal-breakers the person you are dating might have. If you're both in it for a fling, then you needn't worry, but if you might really like a guy and he has stringent non-negotiables, you should be aware that he may not be taking you seriously if you don't fit the bill. I have a male friend who only wants to marry a nice Jewish woman—a woman converting to Judaism for him won't even make the cut. He dates non-Jewish girls and breaks up with them after three months so that he doesn't get too attached or lead them on due to his desires to marry another Jewish person. As I write this, he still is not married to a Jewish woman and has had more short-term casual girlfriends than I can count.

When you find this ideal partner who ticks all your *should* boxes and you are still not happy, you'll begin to question if the desired qualities on your *shoulds* list have been the right ones for you. This is where experience with partners, both sexually and emotionally, will help ensure you pick someone for the right reasons. Experience different qualities men have to offer so you know which ones you enjoy the most and which fit with who you are deep down, not ones you thought you had to tick off a list. My high school boyfriend was perfect on paper— he could tick off every box on any list—but he wasn't perfect *for me*.

I do think it can be helpful to have some criteria to help you as you pick and choose whom to spend time with, but it's important that such criteria for a date or a potential partner come from the right state of mind. Make sure you've explored the qualities you think you want instead of just accepting them; challenge them and test them out. When you care about meaningful qualities in your date—rather than choosing him based on his height, paycheck or clothes or if male-pattern baldness runs in his family (superficial dating)—then you are more likely to have enjoyable dating experiences. The one important quality when dating someone, especially in the SBD world, is *how they make you feel.*

In the past, there were times when the people I chose to be in relationships with and have casual dates with all met certain criteria, inspired by my sexual fantasies and thoughts on the "ideal" man. I was still somewhat open-minded—but more on the "somewhat" side. Many of the attributes I was looking for were exterior ones—I admit I was dating superficially. When I met Matt, not only did he not satisfy my criteria or wish list, he was on the other extreme: covered in tattoos and piercings (which would have given my father a heart attack), he was at a different stage of life (divorced with a child), was from a different religious background (Jehovah's Witness, while I'm Jewish) and was more than a few years older than me (he was over 40, while at the time I was 26). However, I felt fireworks when I caught up with him one day over lunch. The first time we locked lips, the attraction was instant, and without an in-depth discussion, we found ourselves together all the time, enjoying each other's company and experiencing mind-blowing sexual chemistry that was definitely more than just a superficial attraction. And yet, on paper, he was everything wrong for me. As the saying goes, *when you know, you know.* There is no logical explanation, mathematical equation or even words to describe it when something is just right and just works. Sometimes the attraction is simply based on how someone makes you feel when you are with them. It didn't end up working out with Matt in the end, but not because of any deal-breakers or failure to satisfy my dating wish list—more to do with timing.

Even though in the SBD world you might only be looking for casual dates, mini-relationships and hookups, challenging the dating wish list and keeping an open mind is still something you should practice. It can ensure that your dates and hookups are more rewarding (although when it comes to a casual hookup, I'm sure looks and superficial sexual attraction will do every so often) and will also help you get into the right frame of mind if you eventually do decide to date with a future in mind. Being able to judge someone not on their external qualities but based on how they treat you and make you feel is a mature way of dating—something you might only achieve through experience and experimentation.

Exercise—The Dating Wish List

In a column, write five superficial things that are on your dating wish list; for example, what a person looks like, how much money they make or what kind of car they drive. In another column, write five things about how you want a person to make you feel. Now write a number next to each one of these 10 items (from 1 to 10, 1 being the most important thing on your dating wish list and 10 being the least important). I encourage you to try to put as many feelings toward the top of your list as you can and challenge what role any superficial things play and how they benefit you when you are dating or in a relationship.

Superficial Qualities   1–10

_____   _____

_____   _____

_____   _____

_____   _____

_____   _____

How the Person Makes You Feel   1–10

_____   _____

_____   _____

_____   _____

_____   _____

_____   _____

Spoiler Alert: You Are Not Cinderella

When I ask you to challenge the qualities you want in a man and where those ideas come from, you may find some of them come from stories you were told as a child, without your being aware of their impact. Mothers and fathers (and even children's books and movies) tell all little princesses what love and relationships should be like. These underlying messages have most likely become second nature to you and have made you believe that the desire you have for a particular type of man (a prince) is your choice—but the ideas in your head had to come from somewhere.

I am a hopeless romantic, and I do believe in happy endings (get your mind out of the gutter!), but I also believe in a balance between reality and fantasy and so should you. The fairytale fantasy (meet Prince Charming, get married, have two children, a dog and a house with a white picket fence) is a version of the *should* curse. But in this case, it's not only the masses that reinforce this idea but a universal desire for so-called perfection. At some point, the fairytale is no longer about a princess in a castle surrounded by dragons who is saved by a prince, but about a real-life woman, who is also saved, but this time it's by a particular kind of guy, with a particular job, who looks a particular way and is holding out a diamond ring. (Please note that marrying a man does not save you. It might add something special to your life, but "saving" implies that a woman who is single is in some sort of trouble without a man. This is not the case.)

You also need to be careful that you do not mask the reality of your current dating scenarios with the fairytale fables. Women can be overly optimistic, which isn't always a bad thing, but sometimes we choose to believe the fairytale version of what we think we see in front of us when it comes to men, instead of looking at the facts. We also sometimes think that any sign of interest or attention (even sexual) from a guy must mean he likes us.

At a friend's birthday one year, I received attention from this gorgeous-looking guy and we really seemed to hit it off. And he was Jewish! (I could satisfy my physical attraction and desire for a nice Jewish boy all in one!) After a few cocktails and a lot of flirting, the question came whether we should go back to mine for more drinks. Admittedly, I started the night on a bit of a low self-esteem wise (so perhaps was a bit susceptible), but was now very taken by him and I felt I couldn't say no. It was one of those situations where I was convinced that if anything did happen, I would hear from him again, as he was already making future plans for us to catch up. Not only did I never hear from him again, but he left to "move his car" during our drinking and hookup session, and never actually came back! I fell asleep on the couch waiting for him (half-naked) and found out he had kicked on to another party. The message was clear: he was there for one thing and left once he got it. I thought his flirtation meant there might be something more, but I was clearly overly optimistic—and felt quite silly afterward.

It's not just us who tend to see our dating reality through fairytale filters—our female friends are just as guilty, at times telling us what they think we want to hear instead of the uncomfortable truth. (These are the same women who will jump to call a guy you're seeing a bastard when he slips up so that you feel better.)

See reality, accept it and just be pleasantly surprised if things do change and you become the exception.

I want you to also rethink being labeled or called a princess. It can certainly be fun sometimes to be someone's princess, but it's worth a little investigation as to how that word is being used. If you want to use royal labels, why not be a queen? A woman who is worshipped has power and is the one in control, not the one who is being controlled.

The Sex and Dating Bucket Lists

Whether you want to one day be in a monogamous relationship or whether you feel that time and youth are on your side and have not considered the future, think about what is on your sex and dating bucket lists. Then, just like with our dating wish lists, we need to challenge our sex and dating bucket lists.

For a dating bucket list, maybe you've always wanted to try dating multiple people at the same time or have never had sex on the first date, but are curious to see what that would feel like. Maybe you want to try online dating for the first time. For your sex bucket list, have you always wanted to have a threesome or just sleep with another woman? Try anal sex or go to a bondage club? Role-play? The sky is the limit.

You are allowed to desire whatever you want to desire, but if you're going to put together a realistic bucket list, the contents of which will fulfill you, it's important you challenge how each dating desire or sexual activity made the cut. Was it something you saw in a movie or porn? Was it something your best friend did and told you about so now you want to do it, too? Is it an innate desire or did it come from an external influence? If you do want to tick off most of your sex and dating bucket lists, it's important to think of things that you realistically and truly do want to try or experiment with, and that you actually think are possible to do. Having regrets can be the undoing of a good relationship, especially if those regrets have to do with something on your list that in reality would not have made you feel content and happy or leave you feeling positively anyway. Would you be willing to lose a good thing or have feelings of resentment for something that, when you tried it, didn't feel like you expected it would?

Exercise—Sex and Dating Bucket Lists

It's time to make your very own sex and dating bucket lists. In two columns (one for dating and the other for sex), write down all the things you think you might want to try. Just like with the *should do* curse, write at the end of each one where it came from, noting that the ones that came from "self" (as opposed to media, friends, etc.) should be the ones you pay more attention to. Next to each item, write a score of 1-10 as to how likely you think each is to be achieved. Some might be more like fantasies but are still good to include on your list. Circle five things on each list to give yourself a more attainable goal and somewhere to start (too many options can be overwhelming). The goal is not to complete the list entirely, but it's useful to at least identify what should be on there, just in case.

Sex Bucket List	Where Did This Come From?	1–10

_____   _____   _____

_____   _____   _____

_____   _____   _____

_____   _____   _____

_____   _____   _____

_____   _____   _____

_____   _____   _____

Dating Bucket List   **Where Did This Come From?**   **1–10**

_____   _____   _____

_____   _____   _____

_____   _____   _____

_____   _____   _____

_____   _____   _____

_____   _____   _____

_____   _____   _____

_____   _____   _____

_____   _____   _____

_____   _____   _____

That Damn Biological Clock

One option for women who are looking for more time is getting their eggs frozen (something called "nonmedical egg freezing"). For the average SBD woman like you and me, who is trying to balance out this life and the urge and desire for motherhood, we need to know realistically what we are looking at in terms of our fertility timeframe, what we can do to extend it and if freezing our eggs is the simple answer it appears to be.

To get some simple answers to these complex questions, I turned to California-based fertility expert Dr. Aimee Eyvazzadeh for advice. One crucial piece of advice from Dr. Aimee, which I hope you take to heart no matter your age, is that if women check their fertility just like we check cholesterol, a lot of the fear and problems around fertility could be resolved proactively instead of reactively during a crisis.

Q. What are some of the biggest issues with fertility for women these days?

A. Ovarian aging is the biggest fertility issue that women

face. We spend most of our fertile lives trying to avoid getting pregnant, and in today's society, it's quite common to want to try for your first baby over 35. Sadly, the time one wants to start a family may be the right time from a social standpoint but not in line with what's going on with your biological clock.

When asked, many millennials say that they don't ever want to have biological children. They list: not having enough money because of all their debt, not wanting to pass on psychological issues and not being equipped to care for a child. Taylor Swift was even quoted in her early 20s as saying she never wanted kids. But things change for people over time. What may feel right now may be totally different 10 years or 15 years later.

My own sister swore she never, ever wanted kids. At the age of 32, she still said she didn't want kids. I froze her eggs. At 37, she met her life mate and everything changed! She now has two children.

Q. What can we do to prepare for fertility and potential fertility issues?

A. The first time you get your Pap smear, get your hormone levels checked. Do an infertility risk factor assessment. If your mom had infertility, your sisters needed IVF, you have a family history of endometriosis or if you had a fertility gene test that was positive for early menopause, you should be hyperaware about your fertility. Even if you aren't aware or concerned about your fertility, make sure to get your levels checked once in your early 20s, then every five years. At 30, if you are not ready to start your family, get your levels checked every two to three years. Here's the thing: your fertility is best when your levels are good. Consider egg freezing when you have healthy eggs. We shouldn't be waiting for our levels to get worse in order to make a decision to freeze eggs.

Q. Does being on birth control have an effect on fertility?

A. No, but birth control pills mask infertility. They prevent a woman from knowing if she's running out of eggs before it's too late because you still have regular cycles on birth control pills. Then, when women stop their pills, their periods are irregular and they're told that the birth control pills need to "wash out" of their system. There's no such thing. If your periods are irregular after you stop the birth control pill, it may not be related to the birth control and it should be evaluated by a doctor.

Q. At what age should we start to consider egg freezing?

A. Most of my patients in their 40s wish they had frozen their eggs in their 20s! And with the divorce rate the way it is, many patients come to me with their new husbands wanting an option to parent with their new husbands without using donor eggs, but they have to use donor eggs because they have run out of viable eggs.

Women are waiting longer and longer to start their families only because they aren't ready to parent when they're most fertile (20s and early 30s).

It's hard for women in their 20s to think of themselves as having a baby when they're "so old" in their 40s. When you're 40 and just starting your family, you think of yourself as full of energy, but a 20-year-old says, "I would never, ever have kids when I'm that old." But most 40-year-olds are definitely feeling young enough to parent starting at age 40. So, being proactive can save your future self a lot of headaches.

Q. What are the most important things women need to know about egg freezing?

A. Egg freezing is a powerful technology that will give women fertility options when their options may have run out or their chances of pregnancy are lower. It will help women have a larger family when they want and if they want.

- It works. The media seems to have a very slanted view of the true success rates. I've seen articles written saying that chances of pregnancy are only 2 percent and most don't get pregnant with their frozen eggs. Well, that's not true unless you're freezing your eggs over the age of 40.
- The technology has evolved tremendously over the past 10 years with the use of vitrification technology (which is now considered the gold standard).
- Every woman starting a family should know about egg freezing. If you are over 35 and want more than one child, think about egg freezing so that you have options when you're trying for baby number two. Your fertility levels now just mean you have a certain percentage chance of pregnancy now. They don't mean that you will get pregnant and they don't mean that you will also get pregnant two years from now. Patients often ask me, "Can I wait? Do my levels tell me I can wait two years?" I can't tell anyone that.
- Freezing your eggs when your fertility levels are low is still giving you a chance for pregnancy in the future, but ideally women are freezing good eggs when they are younger and more fertile.

Even though it seems like there are egg-freezing stories in the media practically every single day, the message isn't somehow getting to all women that they should consider egg freezing.

Q. What is the egg-freezing landscape in the US?

A. Egg freezing is very popular in the US. Women are thinking about their fertility and getting their fertility levels checked more than ever. Companies are covering it under insurance for employees, women are taking advantage of the technology and also, more than ever, women are choosing the love of a child over the love of a partner. Since women have a fertile window, they're not waiting to parent until they find a partner. They're realizing that if they want to parent with their own eggs, they can do that, then find a partner later.

Q. What are the most important things every woman needs to know about fertility?

A.
1. It doesn't last forever. There is a very short period of time that a woman can start a family. Men don't have that problem—that can father as long as they're still making sperm.
2. Your eggs can't be rejuvenated. When you're ready to have a baby, don't think that you can rely on an IVF doctor to guarantee you a baby. IVF doctors are scientists and they are limited by science. Right now, we can only work with eggs that a patient has. We cannot create better/healthier eggs. Not yet at least. I hope one day that we can!

3. Birth control pills mask infertility. Get your levels checked every year.

4. Cigarettes and other nicotine-containing products are egg-killers. Tobacco products are toxic to your precious eggs.

5. Avoid sexually transmitted diseases as much as you can. An exposure to chlamydia can block your fallopian tubes. An exposure to high-risk HPV can result in you needing a surgery to remove a portion of your cervix that can result in an increased risk of preterm delivery.

6. Look at your environment. Try to avoid environmental toxins as much as possible like lead, well water and plastics.

7. Your fertility isn't skin deep. It doesn't matter how awesome you look on the outside. Exercising and eating right is a great way to give yourself the best chance of having the healthiest pregnancy once you are pregnant, but how you look on the outside isn't related to what's going on with your eggs. Just because you look and feel young doesn't mean at age 47 that your eggs will be viable.

8. #GetAheadOfInfertility, become fertility aware, get your levels checked and live as healthy a life as possible.

Two months shy of my 30th birthday, I decided to freeze my eggs. It was something I had always wanted to do, and the best way I can explain my reasoning is that I was planning for an uncertain future. At a young age, I was in a serious long-term relationship and never considered not having children or that I might one day struggle with fertility. After that relationship ended at age 23 and I started to travel, enjoy my single life and have fun, I got to a stage where I couldn't be certain that children would naturally be a certainty, but I still wanted the option. I let go of my own fairytale as to how I wanted to have children and how many I wanted to have. You don't know where life will lead you or what the circumstances will bring, but the idea of having eggs in the freezer felt like it would give me peace of mind.

Soon after the procedure, I felt different. I felt more relaxed, I became calm and I was able to start focusing on the now instead of worrying about my future, not just around having children but even in other areas in my life.

Dating became different, because it was as though I wasn't in so much of a rush. Even though I was supposed to be an open-minded sexologist, I admit I used to analyze if the person I was dating would be good for a future relationship and could be a father and husband figure. After egg freezing, I started just focusing on who they were right now and how they made me feel. I was present and calm, something I'm not sure I had ever been. Egg freezing is not a guarantee at all, but I felt as though I had a little more time to work it all out.

If you do think you want children at some point, just make sure to be aware of what's going on in your reproductive system. It doesn't have to be scary; as Dr. Aimee says, women should be checking their fertility as normally and often as they check their cholesterol.

No Children, No Marriage, No Problem

I have often thought about how much easier dating would be if I never wanted kids or a husband (and could go through life dating whomever I wanted without having to consider the future), but apparently, that may not actually be so simple. Shelly Horton, a journalist who has become well known for her desire not to have children, told me, "It can make things harder, because at some point you might have to inform your date that not having children is what you want. This is a balancing act of wanting to be honest and not wanting to waste his time if he does, but also not appearing that you see the relationship as something that it is not by discussing a future topic like this too soon." I hadn't considered that talking about not wanting to have kids would be just as complicated as a discussion about wanting to have them. And just as some men might go running if you talk about your desire for kids too soon, as Shelly tells me, "So do some men when you tell them you don't want kids."

My close friend Sarah does not want either marriage or children and has come up with her own concept: expiration dating. To me, this is the ultimate level of mindful dating and Sarah maintains that it makes her life easier. The idea behind expiration dating is that every relationship she is in has an end date. That does not mean she doesn't believe in long-term or committed relationships, but rather that she knows when she enters a relationship that it will end one day. When you think about the fact that, in the US, there is a divorce approximately every 36 seconds (according to statistics from the CDC), maybe putting an expiration date on a relationship ahead of time makes sense. Maybe, this way, there is less pressure to stick it out under the wrong circumstances. Some people believe in one true love; others believe we have many loves throughout our lives. For Sarah, there is no pressure to stay in a relationship: both people are there because they are happy to be there, and they both know it's not forever. In her words, "You can love someone for the pure pleasure of it and not because you are legally bound to." In the US, the marriage rate is currently going down, so it's possible that more people are actually living their lives like this—expiration dating or in expiration marriages—except they don't know this is what they are doing, and the expiration comes as a surprise. Would it be less hurtful if you knew the end of a relationship was inevitable?

Commitment Phobia

Commitment phobia is something I believe we all suffer from in some variation. I know I have personally worked to overcome it in my own life.

Because of increasing options and the rise of "FOMO" (fear of missing out) exacerbated by social media, we are fearful and confused about how to choose just one person. In the SBD world, this is not necessarily a phobia of long-term commitment, but it still indicates that there is pressure to choose someone to continue seeing, even just casually. While some people might view the SBD lifestyle itself as a phobia of commitment, there is a difference between experimenting with an open mind in the dating world and the inability to date one guy due to fear of picking the wrong one or missing out on someone else who may be just around the corner.

If you challenge and analyze the list of qualities you look for in a partner, won't you then have a better chance at finding someone you actually want? That fear of choosing the wrong person doesn't have to be a fear anymore. Experiencing an SBD life means experimenting with different kinds of men and that could be a cure for commitment phobia in longer-term relationships. Once you have tried and tested and become sure of what you want in a partner, you decrease the fear of committing to the wrong person because you also reduce the chances of committing to the wrong person. An SBD woman is on a wise journey because she is working out what she wants in the smartest way possible—with research and firsthand experience.

Chapter 2

I Love Me

The most beautiful thing you can wear is confidence.
—Blake Lively

*Confidence is going after Moby Dick in a rowboat
and taking the tartar sauce with you.*
—Zig Ziglar

As an SBD woman, you will be faced not only with opinions and influences from the external world but also by judgments from within your own mind that may try telling you (in new and more immediate ways) that you are not good enough. In order to avoid thoughts like these impacting your dating— so you can choose men whom you want to date rather than dating just to validate yourself—confidence is your best weapon. Being a confident dater means having the strength to make your own choices regardless of what others think or say because you know they are right for you. Your confidence and self-esteem will influence every choice you make: whom you date, how you date them, how your date makes you feel, whom you will or won't sleep with and even how many sexual partners you'll have.

If you are a people-pleaser, this section on confidence may sound familiar to you. In the pursuit of people-pleasing, you might be putting up with behavior or attitudes that go against your morals and values. A people-pleaser might find herself dating a guy for longer than she should because she enjoys his approval or, when dating someone, not speaking up for herself because she is scared he might walk away. A people-pleaser does not need to accept every guy's romantic or sexual interest just because his interest is the one thing that is appealing to her inner sense of self-worth. Often women who are people-pleasers have a deep-seated fear of rejection. But should we be scared of rejection by men who were not right for us in the first place? If we can achieve a healthy level of confidence and self-esteem, then rejection will go from a real fear to something that rolls off our backs when and if we face it.

When your confidence is high, you are able to choose men to date and have sex with based on real values and feelings that matter, not because you are in search of something to boost your self-esteem.

It's important to be authentically confident in order to make these decisions from a positive and empowered state of mind. If you try to gain confidence through dating and sex, you may find that the short-lived positive effects pale in comparison with the more severe, long-term negative consequences.

Confidence is inextricably linked to our body image and sense of self-worth. Although I am a strong woman who believes in herself, I have struggled with both. There are days that I can't avoid self-doubt rushing into my every thought. Even so, I know that being strong does not mean never feeling this way; being strong is about knowing how to pick yourself up no matter how shitty you are feeling. The more confidence you have, the less likely you are to give into negative thought patterns.

When you are an SBD woman in a modern world, you are often forced to step outside your comfort zone. At times you may feel inadequate due to the lack of an "official" partner and the unsolicited comments that come with it. Some of your dating and sexual experiences might also test your self-esteem. It is a fight between these external influences and the way we choose to deal with them in our heads. Be patient with yourself: external influences—particularly the constant, inescapable nature of social media—have quite a bit of ammo and *will* test you.

Like anything, social media also has upsides and advantages, but what I want SBD women to heed is the "my life is better than yours" game we see on many social media platforms and how that might impact their dating, sex and love choices. Images of people that are passed off as reality in actuality take so much work to set up and facilitate and are used to show a standard that is not natural or even attainable. You've heard of selfies, but now we are seeing more of the "relfie"—the relationship selfie. Is the relationship pictured really all smiles? Has this relationship really made the couple complete, as it aims to show? If you are not able to live up to these so-called "real" relationships you see on social media, how does that make you feel? Like you are not good enough? Does it make you doubt your own relationship choices?

The best way to combat negative self-image—whether induced by unrealistic standards of self or relationships in the media or not—is to focus on doing things that make you feel good. If you love to cook, exercise or have wine with friends, do more of that! If you love to spend time in nature or go to the movies, do more of that!

Exercise—Positive Media

In one column, list the type of media you consume, whether it be TV, magazines or influences on social media. In the next column, use just one adjective to describe how the source you listed makes you feel. Look at the sources next to which you listed a *positive* adjective. Remember them—they empower you! This is the sort of messaging that should populate your feed/magazine stand/television. Next to any of the sources that make you feel an adjective that is *negative,* write an action down that you can do to combat that negativity—that may be unfollowing the account, not watching that show, unfriending that person on Facebook or buying a different magazine. If you have few or no positive adjectives for the media you consume, try to investigate media that does give you a positive feeling. You might need to ask friends or search on the internet. We can always combat negativity with something positive.

Media	Adjective	Action
_____	_____	_____
_____	_____	_____
_____	_____	_____

_____   _____   _____

_____   _____   _____

_____   _____   _____

Friends and Family

Maybe you were brought up to believe that a woman should look or act in a particular way—these are most likely ideas put into your head by family members. When you don't live up to these standards, which may have come from old-fashioned ideals or cultural beliefs, you can be left feeling less confident. You may have been criticized for your appearance or weight growing up, or been compared with a sibling. While your family thought this was a way to show you love or motivate you to change, it can have an entirely different, more negative effect.

When you sit around talking with friends about how terrible you feel, it can bring a certain comfort: misery loves company and sharing similar stories shows us that we are not the only ones who doubt ourselves. But there is a point at which this complaining becomes toxic, and past that point, negative talk will only cause you more harm, sending you spiraling further into self-doubt. Talk things out with friends and support each other, but recognize when that is no longer helpful and start empowering each other to start thinking differently. Wallowing in self-pity won't get you anywhere.

Some women genuinely need the support of their friends,

and if you have a friend like that, offer a helping hand. However, some women can be too self-critical, and complain not because they need support, but because they need constant validation from other people. In this case, your support may only be enabling their self-critical view and it could rub off on your own mood and thoughts. This is the difficult balance between being a good friend and knowing when someone else's energy is harmful. Dealing with this is not always a matter of eliminating that person from your life, but at least acknowledge that this transference is there and challenge it. Also, try to spend more time with those who inspire you. Just as negative attitudes rub off, so do positive ones. Optimism and a healthy self-esteem are sexy, too.

Clear the Decks

Many of us are very sensitive to the influences around us and within us, so it's important to take control and change things that negatively affect your self-esteem. Sometimes simply identifying and challenging the negative influences in your life can be enough to bring your self-esteem back to a healthy point. Other times, you need to go a step further.

Step back for a moment and choose to eliminate those negative influences in your life at least while you work on yourself. You have a choice in what you read, whom you follow, what you watch on TV, whom you spend time with, where you shop and what designers you wear. Start a chain reaction of positivity in your life by understanding that you are the gatekeeper to your own life and you decide what messages are allowed to come through.

Focusing again on social media: just as I would not let every person into my home, I would also not let them into my personal and private online world. The "block" and "unfriend" options are your new best friends. You have the power to eliminate lots of toxicity at the push of a button.

Social media (and technology in general) can be harmful to your mental health in more ways than self-esteem. Be mindful of what you are posting and how much time you are spending with your face behind a screen. It can take up far too much of your thought processes, considering every detail of what you wear, what filter you use and where you will go in order to get that one great shot. Instead of enjoying interactions during a get-together, you can become distracted, multitasking between managing social media and holding a conversation for which you can't be present. Practice putting your phone down and living presently and mindfully in the moment.

If you are feeling that you are stuck in a bit of a life rut, everything lacking luster and causing you to feel that the world is falling down around you (believe me, I have been there!), paring down those you follow on social media or the time you spend behind a screen in general can impact your mindset immensely. Whether the problem is how you feel about yourself, job stress, a dwindling social life or something different, the positive step of weeding out messaging from our lives that isn't helpful is a great start.

You need to be aware of the difference between interaction with a factor that negatively impacts your self-esteem and actual psychological issues such as depression and anxiety, which can also play a big part in these kinds of life ruts. If the latter is your case, a therapist can be a really positive tool. You may have lived through situations in your past that you never completely recovered from, the effects of which are still doing a negative dance in your subconscious. If you suspect that your harmful thoughts are coming from something deep within, then I strongly suggest you seek professional help. I sought counseling to help with my self-esteem and discovered that there were issues from my past I hadn't even realized were making me feel the way I did. You can't eliminate all negativity from your life, but you can learn how to be responsible for the way you react to it and minimize the impact.

"I Think I Can, I Think I Can..."

Once you have eliminated or taken a break from certain things, it's time to increase your best tool—a positive attitude. Challenging the messages and beliefs from outside influences is one way to change your attitude, but turning the focus from a negative to a positive one is the next step.

Cultivating a positive attitude is about changing the way we see ourselves and where our thoughts go. When our eyes meet our body in our reflection in the mirror, most of our attention goes straight to the things that we don't like or that we want to change. We automatically begin to criticize. Why spend all that time thinking about what you don't like (especially when your dislike might be born of unrealistic standards programmed by society or social media), when you could be focusing on what you love and celebrating yourself?

Changing your outlook is an ongoing process, but there are some great ways to get that process started. It really comes down to a choice: do you want to focus on the negative or do you want to learn how to love and accept yourself? I see it as a switch in our heads: sit there and complain—or worship and love. It doesn't mean that you do not want to change things in your life or work on your body or health, but it means you do it out of love for yourself, not hatred. As much as it might not feel like it sometimes, we all have the choice in life to be negative or positive. We *can* control our mood instead of our mood controlling us.

We also need to consider that when we are dating with a negative mindset, we will carry that bad attitude with us on dates, judging the person sitting in front of us as negatively as we do ourselves and focusing on what they are not instead of what they are. Seeing someone through those judgmental eyes is a sure way to risk undeservedly dismissing someone great.

> *It sounds like a cliché, but I learnt that you're not going to fall for the right person until you really love yourself and feel good about who you are.*
> —Emma Watson

Exercise—Positive Mirror Work

This exercise will require a mirror. Women usually tend to look in the mirror and see what they don't like or want to change. This exercise is about focusing on and highlighting the things you love about yourself. This is also a good exercise for switching your mind from negative to positive.

Every morning for the next week, I want you to look in the mirror and, from head to toe, go through your body parts and say to yourself all the things you love. These could be things like the color of your eyes or the length of your neck.

At the end of that week, on a piece of paper, in your phone or even in this book, write a positive statement about yourself. Positive affirmations were something I always felt awkward about, but during a time when my self-esteem was tenuous at best, I found they really helped. An example is "I am a strong and confident woman who is beautiful inside and out and can achieve whatever I put my mind to." Any positive affirmation that feels right to you will do. Place the affirmation somewhere you will see it often or read it each morning before you start your day, saying it repeatedly out loud (I always say mine five times in a row!) to cement it in your brain.

_____

_____

_____

_____

_____

Exercise—Gratitude

Another great exercise to do at the end of each day is to write down three things that you are grateful for. I once purchased a small exercise book that had this in it and I found it really helped me. Write the date on top, as it can be useful to go back and have a reminder of all the great things that happened in that week. We tend to slip back into negative thoughts not only about ourselves but about the situations we find ourselves in. End the day focusing on what is good and hopefully carrying that on to the next.

_____

_____

_____

The Man Ban

If you feel that you are dating or sleeping with men purely for the attention or if you are not quite sure whether this is the case, you can discover this on a "man ban." This means taking the men out of your life (no dates, no sex and minimal phone contact) in order to work out not only what role they might have but also what issues you might be using them to mask.

Men can be a lot of fun, but they can also be energy-draining distractions, and you might need that energy to work through your own problems and challenges. How will you know if the television shows and magazines you watch and read affect your body confidence if you keep using the attention of men to mask their negative effects?

Sometimes it's good to take a step back and have a break so you can see your life with fresh eyes. Take the time on your man ban to do all the things you need to do to build yourself up as a stronger woman. I went on a man ban while writing this book and, as much as I also needed the extra time and energy, it taught me once again about the men in my life and the reason each is there.

A man ban is also a good time to "masturdate"—enjoy and pleasure yourself in a nonsexual way. Date yourself: do nice things for yourself, pamper yourself with a beauty treatment, a weekend trip or a splurge on a new outfit—and enjoy your own company in the process.

The man ban allows you to do exactly what you want without having to consider anyone's needs but your own (single doesn't sound so bad now, does it?). That can be very therapeutic and beneficial for a busy SBD woman and it also gives you time to recharge, rebuild and work on self-love.

Exercise—The Man Ban

In order to have an effective man ban, you'll need to set a time period. Your man ban could be for a number of weeks, until a work project is done, until you reach a state of emotional contentment or some other goal. While on your man ban, it's important to set challenges, the overcoming and achieving of which will make you feel good about yourself and prove that you are stronger than you think. Pick a couple of the below, or come up with your own:

- **Health:** Getting fit and healthy is not about weight loss but feeling truly healthy from the inside out. This was the focus during my own man ban. Even more than physically, changing my routines to be my best self was a great mental challenge. It helped to have something so positive to focus on.

- **Sport:** Taking on a physical challenge is a great way to prove to yourself you are capable of doing something that your mind might doubt you can. This could be training for a (half-) marathon or taking up a sport you've never tried before.

- **Education:** Since you have some time on your hands, maybe there is a new skill you want to pick up, a course you want to take or even a new language you want to learn. Not only is this intellectually stimulating, but it is a great way to mix with some new people for when you do want to re-enter the dating world. After one breakup, I decided to learn to speak French and it has led me on many trips to Paris to use those skills.

- **Socializing:** Set yourself the goal of spending time with people you might not have seen in a while or reconnecting with people who will enrich your life. We often talk about catching up but many times it never happens. During your man ban is a great time to reconnect with some of these worthy people.

Time Frame

_____

Challenges to Overcome/Goals to Achieve

_____

_____

_____

Bringing Down the Wall

There is a term that I loathe but that is important for any SBD woman to get their head around: *intimidating.* I get asked all the time, "Isn't it intimidating for men to date you?" My job as a sexologist is intimidating for some men, but those are the kind of men I don't date, so it's a great filtering process.

Women have put ourselves out there in the world on the same platforms as men, and while there are hugely positive impacts of this, it has also opened our lives to criticism and potential harm in our professional, emotional or romantic lives. This is why some women build a wall around them like a fort, to protect themselves. A strong female persona can be deemed intimidating because she is already anticipating a battle and is therefore on guard at all times. We need to question if it's really possible to get to know someone, connect with them and allow them to know the best version of us if we have a fort built around who we really are.

Don't be scared of being vulnerable and potentially opening yourself up to pain. The brilliant author Brené Brown has a great quote that says, "We cultivate love when we allow our most vulnerable and powerful selves to be deeply seen and known." Life is about taking risks and being hurt is often how we grow and what furthers us on our paths to love. This is yet another reason why healthy self-esteem and having the strength to be a confident dater are paramount: if you know how to pick up the pieces when things don't work out, then being vulnerable is not so scary. Vulnerability itself is not about being weak or opening yourself up to pain; it is about showing up despite risk and being open to having real and honest connections with people. That vulnerable energy can also be seen as feminine energy, and let me tell you, it can be a real turn-on.

SOS! What's Your Emergency Plan?

Your brain is your bitch.

—Jen Sincero

We all have bad days when, for whatever reason, it feels like the entire world is against us. The trick to being prepared for these times is to have an emergency plan.

When it happens, take your time and have your sad moment. Crying can be good; so can chocolate and a chick flick. Maybe try a pampering quick fix or read a certain passage that always pulls you out of the depths. Know your emergency plan, because life can't ever really pull you down if you know how to pull yourself back up.

Your emergency plan will especially come in handy when you have to handle rejection. Rejection is a part of (the SBD) life—and there are ways to make it easier to handle, such as not internalizing it and resisting the impulse to wonder if it's something we did that caused it. Many times we will never know definitively what caused a rejection, and we need to accept that—especially in the SBD world, where an honest reason for not calling back might not be entirely required.

Rejection hurts. Just keep working on being a confident dater, so someone's rejection of you might only hurt briefly, and practice picking yourself up when you are down. There is strength in knowing how to get back to that place of confidence when you lose it momentarily. If all else fails, remember: rejection eventually serves you. Sometimes you are "rejected" by something because the universe is steering you away from something that would have been toxic for you or opening the door to something even better. You may not feel it in the moment, but one day you will look back on every perceived rejection and know the reason for it in your life.

Exercise—Break in Case of an Emergency

When you are really feeling down, it's hard to think about what it is that will for sure get you on your feet. For these times, you need a tangible reminder of your feel-good tactics. Write a list of things that you can do that you *know* will bring you out of a negative mood. You can include people who you know would be willing to assist you during those times. It's useful to write these down so when you are feeling low, the thinking has been done for you.

_____

_____

_____

Practice Dating

We are not really taught how to date; most of us are just going in blind, trying to work it out along the way. Just like learning how to ride a bike, it's important to start with training wheels—*practice dating*.

This idea of dating someone purely for practice and without any intention to develop feelings may sound harsh, and in truth, it does run the risk of hurting others' emotions, but I believe the benefits of practice dating outweigh those risks.

When we take dating seriously, we also take seriously the men we choose, but if it's just a practice run, you really need only choose someone who intrigues you enough to sit through a meal with. When you know it's only a practice round, you might be able to relax more and go with the flow—which, ironically, is the right frame of mind to be in when you are on a proper date, too. We can also learn something from the way we choose men in the practice dating field, as opening up our minds to more men for intrigue's sake can result in surprises around qualities we never thought we would accept, like or want in a partner.

Practice dating is about practicing your dating skills, dealing with nerves and getting used to putting yourself in dating situations. Throw yourself in the deep end and step outside of your comfort zone, so when you do get serious you have some idea of what you're doing and maybe a little more confidence, too.

Practice dating can also be a great way for someone to get their dating confidence back after leaving a relationship, as during a relationship, things can get comfortable and the skills used on dates can get rusty. It's also good to feel desirable again, especially if that last relationship or fling lacked passion and interest. There isn't such a thing as perfection when it comes to dating, but if practice makes perfect, then practice dating might get you close. And who knows whom you might find in your warmup rounds.

Bitch, Please

You don't have to be a bitch to land a man. There is an old saying, "Be mean, keep 'em keen." Taken literally, I really object to this, because it is downright dirty game playing. Unfortunately, though, there is a kernel of truth in what it says about pushing someone away. I would rather the saying went, "Be confident, keep 'em keen," as I feel it's not only just as true but comes from a healthier mindset. In this case, the "be mean" is just having the confidence to stand up for what you want and how you want to be treated. The point is, people are attracted to confident people. Rather than having to play games and push someone away to get them to come running back, it's better to hold your head up high, keep your boundaries tight and attract people because you believe in yourself and they should, too. You might be "mean" to a guy who is not treating you right because you believe in yourself, encouraging him to try again with a more respectful approach. He may want you because you now seem unavailable and not keen. You need to learn the difference between a guy who is genuinely coming back to try again and one who just wants to win you over because it seems like a challenge.

Once you build yourself up into a confident SBD woman who gets her validation from within and who trusts her own strength, why would you let anyone, especially a romantic interest, disrespect you? Anyone who can't see you for the amazing woman you are just doesn't deserve to date or have sex with you. I wish all women would hold that statement close to their hearts. Even in the area of casual sex where you're just having fun, why shouldn't you also be respected? The way that respect is shown is entirely up to you, according to your own morals around what respect looks like for each dating and sexual scenario.

Chapter 3

Let's Talk About Sex, Baby

Women have all the power, because women have all the vaginas.
—Dave Attell

One thing is clear: women are exploring their sexuality outside of committed, monogamous relationships—this tendency to have more casual, uncommitted sexual relationships is known as sociosexuality.

One of the problems with sex in the dating world is defining what it is. According to research from the Kinsey Institute, "no single generation or gender agrees on a definition of 'had sex.'" Does it mean a penis in a vagina? What if you are a same-sex couple? Do oral and anal sex count as sex if they are the ways in which you are intimate with your partner? If you hook up with a guy and only engage in activities that are not penetration, does it mean less because there is no penetration? Do you need to have an orgasm for it to be classified as sex, or does a man need to ejaculate? What happens if you have penis–vagina sex and neither of these occur? It's just as difficult to define what good sex is. Is it frequency, number of orgasms, length of time, a feeling of happiness or laughter, or just all-around pleasure?

Women do not often receive permission when it comes to sex. Permission to know that it's okay to talk about sex, to think about sex, to have sex, to explore sex and to engage in it without love or even a relationship. It has been reported that women can think of sex up to 140 times a day, with an average of 19 times. Having sex with someone you love can be a beautiful experience, but let's get real: sometimes a girl's just gotta get laid! How you decide to engage in that activity and whom you do it with should be up to you, but you should decide these things from the right frame of mind. Sex should be for fun, intimacy, pleasure, connection, love or procreation. If you're doing it for reasons other than these, you may want to rethink your motives.

As far as we have come, there is still a lot of shame attached to our sexual wants and desires as women. This means we need to challenge what we feel is expected of us in order to get the sex life we really want.

Ready to Get Randy

It's work having a vagina. Guys don't think that it's work but it is. You think it shows up like that to the event? It doesn't. Every night it's like getting it ready for its first Quinceañera, believe me.
—Amy Schumer

In the previous chapter, we talked about confidence. Although confidence truly does come from within, I think that keeping your lady bits sex- and dating-ready can help with body confidence and add a little somethin' somethin' to your mojo as you hop from SBD scenario to SBD scenario.

The SBD life can be spontaneous and full of surprises, so I take a better-safe-than-sorry approach to the following body

confidence measures. I always found that when I was least prepared was when things would happen, which meant I was not
as present in the moment; I was more worried about the extra
pubic hair I hadn't waxed than my pleasure or even the person
I was with. There is an easy way to overcome these situations
and guarantee you're able to be present even in the most spontaneous of moments: always be prepared.

Underwear: The reality is that if you're engaging in sexy fun,
your underwear may not be in the picture too long. Either way,
your undies will make a cameo at some point, so you'd best
feel good in them. While control panties can make a dress look
amazing, if there is any chance of a sexual encounter, I recom-
mend you wear a dress that doesn't need them. If you can't have
matching underwear all the time (and who has the time to be
that prepared?), the best bet is to have a lot of plain and colorful G-strings, thongs and more comfortable booty shorts. That
way you always have something to match any bra. Remember,
underwear is not about him; it is about making sure you feel
sexy so you can concentrate on the moment, instead of being
paranoid about what he might think of your granny panties.

Pubic hair: This is such a personal choice. Whatever style
makes you feel the best (a '70s bush, landing strip, bald as the
day you were born, even bejeweled) is great; just try to make
sure it's always groomed. If you prefer a Brazilian but couldn't
make it to the salon this month, have no fear. He will still hook
up with you; the only difference is that you may be preoccu-
pied worrying about it. Being prepared really is more about our
body confidence than about a partner's pleasure.

Feminine hygiene: If it's a hot day and you have been really
sweaty, chances are you'll sweat down there, too, and will be
paranoid if you end up taking your clothes off with someone.

This one is more difficult, as you always leave your home clean but can't control the weather. If you find out it's going to be a scorcher, make sure you wear cotton underwear that can breathe. I was once caught in a heat wave in New York and found myself randomly out on a date. When things took a surprising (and sexy) turn, I snuck off to the bathroom and gave myself a mini-birdbath, just to put my mind at ease.

How your vulva looks: Many women are self-conscious about the way they look down there. The fear of a man thinking they don't look normal can keep them from enjoying the moment and certainly from achieving orgasm. The fact is this: everyone looks different. You need to learn to embrace these differences and love yourself, all of yourself, just the way you are. I once brought this subject up with a man and he told me that, when men are getting lucky, worrying about the shape and size of your labia is the last thing on their mind—they are just happy to be getting lucky! If you are still worried your vulva doesn't look normal, try to expose yourself to images of different vulvas to see the variety (there are book and website resources for this).

Sexual Identity

A woman's sexuality can be fluid, changing throughout her lifespan. This fluidity has implications for the labels we use now and for our future relationships. Working out sexuality can be a complex and lengthy process—we never really stop experimenting with who we are and how we identify ourselves in this world. To really do yourself justice, you must experiment from a place of just being you.

In the case of a woman who occasionally enjoys sex or intimacy with another woman but does not identify as gay or bisexual, we commonly eroticize it, rather than attempt to find a label. It's normal and natural for a woman to want to experiment and have different experiences sexually and romantically with other women, but we are also taught from a young age that girls kissing other girls is appealing to men. If you find yourself with urges you don't understand, try not to label or judge yourself. Simply try to understand where they come from and decide if acting upon these urges resonates with who you really are and feels authentic to you.

One of the biggest judgment problems facing an SBD woman in a modern sexual world is punishment for having "too much" sex and/or sex outside of a monogamous relationship. These negative labels are not just words: they are representations of harmful views toward sexuality. We need to continue to challenge use of words like *slut, whore* and *promiscuous* (any label that describes a woman who supposedly has a lot of sex but does not come with a definitive number of partners in its description). How many people do you actually have to have sex with and what sexual acts do you need to engage in to be labeled this way? Is it just a lot of penis–vagina sex that counts or are blowjobs considered *slutty*, too?

So what if you have had a few men in your life—does it make you any less of a person than someone who has had one or none? Why should someone who hasn't had sex be labeled as pure and innocent and someone with an active sex life be called dirty or made to feel guilty? And what are you guilty of? Being a sexually enthusiastic woman who enjoys the act of sex? Sex is something beautiful, fun and pleasurable when you feel the circumstances are right—not just when you are married or in a monogamous relationship. Once upon a time, there were no such things as condoms, birth control pills or paternity tests, so sexuality was tightly controlled in order for a man to ensure the paternity of his child. We don't live in that era anymore; times have changed and sex is certainly not just about procreation.

These labels that degrade certain sexual choices also imply that there is some benchmark of "normal" when it comes to sex. But if we can't even define what sex is, we can hardly define what is sexually normal. All people are different and likewise our wants are different; at times they are just confused by external influences.

In the SBD world, when you might not be settled down with just one person, these are labels that, unfortunately, you run the risk of hearing. (Why they still exist in a world where we have near-equal rights and female empowerment abounds frustrates me deeply!) Rest assured, they are just a way to control women with fear and shame; these labels are not who you are. If you know that in your bones, then you will be able to shrug off any negativity coming from within your own head or from those around you as you explore and enjoy your SBD life.

Don't Hate, Masturbate!

The principal concern for women is not having an orgasm.
But a woman has to take responsibility for her own orgasms.
—Dr. Ruth Westheimer

The way we view self-pleasuring and masturbation has a lot of parallels to the way we view dating. We are sometimes scared to experiment, unsure of how the process works and often feel like the man is in control of certain things. Just like with self-pleasuring, you need to understand how you like to date (by experimentation, of course) and you should be more in control after understanding what it is you want and what you enjoy.

It's important to work out how to experience sexual pleasure yourself, so you know what you want in sexual encounters with others; self-pleasuring opens up your mind (and other things, too!) to possibilities you may not otherwise have considered. There are no limits with masturbation—no rules or standard moves. Masturbation is simply whatever feels good to you and doesn't have to have a goal or ending in sight. There are also countless healthy benefits (besides feeling amazing), including assisting with sleep, stress and anxiety reduction, mood elevation and many more. I prefer to use the term "self-pleasuring," as masturbating can be heavily associated with a male sexual act ending in orgasm and ejaculation.

There are a couple of important pieces of information that might help on your quest for pleasure. First of all, our genitals should not only be labeled a vagina. A vagina only refers to the vaginal canal, which contains the G-spot and which many women give birth from). We should also be acknowledging the vulva, which is the entire external area and contains many other pleasure points including the clitoris, the source of orgasm for most women.

(That we define female sexuality primarily by vaginal sex used for penetration—and not through these other areas—could be the reason why many women feel unsatisfied in the bedroom.)

Women are taught from an early age that self-pleasuring is not okay. We tolerate boys masturbating and even encourage it—painting it with a comedic slant—but girls are taught not to touch themselves and that their sexuality is a flower to give away to someone else.

By these standards, women are left expecting their partners to know how to pleasure them, and, as every woman is different and desires different things, sex can become a game of failed mind reading, disappointment and boredom. Women who have learned about themselves by self-pleasuring are better equipped to experience that pleasure with another person, as they are able to tell and show their partner what they want and how they work. I had my first orgasm at the age of 21, and I'm pleased to say it was by my own hand. I'd previously thought I had orgasms during penetrative sex with a boyfriend, but please note if you "think" you have had an orgasm, you haven't.

Women who self-pleasure are in more control of their sexual functioning and in turn experience sexual self-confidence that can translate to general self-confidence with dating.

Self-pleasuring might also keep you from having sex with Mr. Wrong. If you know you are able to experience pleasure by your own hands, then there shouldn't be a need to get it from the wrong person. We can't replace men altogether with self-pleasuring, but wouldn't it be better to pleasure ourselves than welcome Mr. Wrong into our bed if Mr. Right Now isn't available?

There is also the struggle for women between their sexual urges and the desire to wait to get to know a person they are dating until they feel safe. This waiting period can have us climbing the walls! Self-pleasuring is a great way to tide us over until we feel comfortable enough to transfer our sexual energy to a new partner.

Sex in the Beginning

In the past, sex was something to look forward to once you were in love. This is still the case in many situations, but it's increasingly common to find sex beginning a relationship. Some people go out to dinner; others will jump straight into bed. It's difficult to know in these undefined scenarios what the right thing to do is, sexually, and it will vary from person to person and situation to situation.

If it is just a casual hookup, you might want to let your hair down and make the most of it, as you never know when it might happen again. If you are dating or building a relationship, you might want to wait a little longer before you unleash your inner sexual goddess, building intimacy as you go (which can help to increase pleasure). Or, you might want to test out the sexual chemistry straight away. Whatever path you choose, there are three important factors to keep in mind: trust, boundaries and consent.

It can be difficult to create trust with someone you might not know very well, but that's why, as women, we need to trust ourselves. You are the one making the decisions and you are the best person to determine what level of trust you need. You should only do sexually what you consent to do without force or intimidation, and it's important to let your partner know what you do and do not consent to. Practicing consent is also about trusting your instincts, as you should never do something you are not comfortable with.

Consent is also about knowing and setting your own boundaries. We all have boundaries when it comes to dating and, especially, to sex. Know what those boundaries are, why they exist and how to protect them (usually by giving or not giving consent). You don't have to cross a boundary just so someone will like you. In the beginning of a relationship, it is natural to want to make a good impression sexually, but make sure that you are only consenting to things that resonate with you and that you will feel good about when it is over.

You also can't expect someone else to be a mind reader and know where your boundaries are if you don't verbalize them. You can't get angry if a partner or date tries to cross your line without being informed it was there in the first place. Just because the SBD world might contain more liberal sexual encounters doesn't mean you shouldn't have boundaries and shouldn't let them be known. As much as you might want to have fun, crazy sexual time, there is nothing wrong with enforcing boundaries, and you have every right to do so.

If someone doesn't respect your boundaries, you know where to tell them to go.

Enthusiasm: The Key to His Heart (And His Crotch)

A lot of dissatisfaction in the bedroom comes from not understanding how bodies—ours and those of our partners—work. The remedy to this is communication: tell your partner what you want and ask them what they want in return, no matter how awkward that can sometimes be. I once interviewed world-famous porn star Ron Jeremy on his tips for women on how to give a good blowjob. I was in total agreement when he informed me that his key tip was enthusiasm. Why do men like enthusiasm? Because they want to know that it isn't a chore for you. Your enjoyment of the act is what turns them on! An SBD woman may be an empowered woman, but there is nothing wrong with wanting to pleasure someone else as long as you're doing it because you enjoy it and not because you feel you have to.

Just like we want him to understand what we want in the bedroom, we should work out what he likes, too. This can be done without asking questions directly. It's simple trial and error, as well as being a good listener. Experiment with different things, different techniques, strokes and hand or body movements. The key is then to read his body language, taking notice of what you are doing and his reactions. He might moan and groan in pleasure, say "yes" or hold you tight or you might feel his body react in a positive way. Does he squirm, do his muscles tense up, is he arching his back? There might be a bit of multitasking involved, but look for the signals. If you are performing oral sex, reach up to his lower abdomen with one hand so you are able to feel when his muscles contract with pleasure. This way you know what to do more or less of and what's working for him. Set a precedent for what you want in the bedroom: if you want enthusiasm and pleasure, give enthusiasm and pleasure.

Exercise—Sexual Boundaries

So many women think they know their sexual boundaries but have never actually taken the time to identify them, write them down and explore why they are there. Write down five boundaries or more that you have when it comes to sex and hooking up. Next to each, write why it is there: how you came to the conclusion or discovered this was your line. For example: I don't like to have sex on the first date—because I very quickly develop connections when I have sex and don't feel that's a safe place if I don't know someone well. Doing this exercise will help you understand why a particular boundary exists and hopefully that understanding will cement it in your behaviors and actions.

Boundary	Why This Boundary Exists

Tip: If you are not sure whether you should have sex with someone, consider these three things:

1. What are the potential consequences?
2. What is your mindset? Are you feeling a bit low about yourself and needing a pick-me-up?
3. What are your feelings for this person? Do you like them and might want to date them later, or is it pure sexual attraction and nothing else?

Love vs. Lust

*Distrust all those who love you extremely upon a very
slight acquaintance and without any viable reason.*
—Lord Chesterfield

The feelings associated with intimacy can be confusing.
When you are spending time with someone in and out of the
bedroom, intimacy is going to occur. Don't be scared of it. In
no way does it mean you are necessarily in love or are meant
to be with that person. Just like sex and love can be amazing
together, you can have sex without love and so too can you
experience the pleasure of intimacy inside and outside of
loving situations.

Becoming intimate with someone involves letting your
guard down, getting emotionally close and allowing someone
to understand how you really feel. It takes confidence and
strength. It's natural that when we have sex, particularly
regular sex with one person, that these feelings will occur.
Our body will release sex hormones such as oxytocin (the
cuddle hormone) that help us to bond with the person we are
having sex with. This can be a lovely feeling to have and also
a great recipe for amazing sex. On top of that, feelings of intimacy can help you relax sexually and more easily achieve an
orgasm.

However, it is imperative to differentiate "hormone bonding"
from "in-love bonding." In-love bonding takes much more to
cultivate. It's nice to bond with someone you are having sex
with, but it doesn't mean you need to be in a relationship with
them. Make sure you can differentiate in yourself feelings

resulting from those damn intense sex hormones (and maybe a little future imagining) and feelings resulting from in-love intimacy. Confusing the two is unfortunately one of the risks of casual sex and dating.

Does Size Matter? That Is the Question

Size shouldn't matter, because 80 percent of women don't even achieve orgasm through vaginal intercourse alone and need help from clitoral stimulation (and since the clitoris is situated outside of the vaginal opening, even a large penis doesn't exactly reach it) and the G-spot is on the upper wall of the vaginal canal, sometimes requiring upward pressure—which many penises do not reach and many sexual positions do not allow him to hit. However, fingers most certainly can!

Some women physically enjoy the sensation of a larger (longer or wider) penis, but that also comes down to how we define what good sex is. An orgasm, the length of time a man can last, the connection between people and a fun time can also be important areas of pleasure. If it's an orgasm you are after, maybe it should matter more what he can do with his fingers and mouth and how open he is to including a vibrator. I think the size debate is just a competitive masculine activity from the locker room that has been passed on to women as a belief. If you find yourself in a position where you are judging a man based on the size of his penis, consider its role in how you achieve an orgasm—externally (clitoris) or internally (G-spot)—and also how you value good sex.

Making Safer Sex Sexy

*Ladies, you sold 200 boxes of Girl Scout cookies as a kid and
now you can't sell a man on wearing a condom? Come on.*
—Dr. Ruth Westheimer

Safer sex is vital to discuss in the SBD world, as you might be
having sex with more than one person or moving between
partners with little time in between. I do not feel that attitudes around testing and general sexual health information
have caught up with our sexual lifestyles, which is even more
reason for you to be the one to take control and be responsible.
The traditional advice—which some people still follow—was
to get tested before each new partner, but what happens if we
are having more than one sexual partner in a weekend? What
happens if you have had a bad experience with a physician—
felt judged for your sexual choices or not free to divulge all the
facts of your activity? Part of being responsible for your own
sexual health is ensuring you have a medical professional you
are comfortable with to discuss sensitive matters.

You need to determine when it's appropriate you get tested,
according to how many different sexual partners you have
had, what sexual acts you've done and what level of protection you've used. According to Dr. Brad McKay, "The best I
can suggest for heterosexual men/women who are also not
in long-term monogamous relationships is to be tested every
three to six months, if asymptomatic. Of course, they should
be tested if they have symptoms, or if a partner says that they
have tested positive for an STI."

Growing up, the acronym STD was taught as something to fear and a reason to either abstain from sex or use a condom. These days we do have a slightly healthier attitude towards sexual health and the way it's discussed, but unfortunately we also have more of a chance at coming into contact with a medical issue due to a sexual encounter. One way we can help protect ourselves is to talk about sexual health issues and become informed and aware. However, it's important when talking about them to be factual and not degrading as you never know the sexual health of those you are speaking with or who might be standing nearby. It's important to use the term STI (Sexually Transmitted Infection) over STD (Sexually Transmitted Disease). When we say the word *disease,* not only does it sound more negative but also the word *disease* implies symptoms. Many common STI's do not have visible symptoms.

It's important to know the facts around what is involved with STIs and to become as knowledgeable as you can. STIs are more common than you think, especially herpes and chlamydia among heterosexual women. STIs don't go with a personality type; you can't tell by looking at someone if they have them, as they often have no symptoms, and you are not always protected from them by using a condom.

Sex will never be entirely safe, which is why we need to start referring to it as *safer* sex. That doesn't mean you should be scared of it—driving can be dangerous but we still do it— but rather be prepared, taking responsibility for your own sexual health. Making safer sex sexy is being in charge, being informed, getting tested, and understanding STIs, how they are transmitted and how to protect yourself; it is about making informed decisions instead of remaining ignorant, which will only put you at a higher risk.

The next best thing you can do is carry your own barrier protection—specifically, condoms. You just never know when you might need one. (There are other forms of barrier protection—such as the female condom and dental dams to be put over the vulva region during oral sex—but condoms are most commonly used and most readily for sale.) There is a higher chance you'll use condoms if you have them with you in the first place and also if they are a kind/brand/style you are comfortable with. If you don't want anyone to know, put them in a smaller purse or container to keep them discreetly hidden. Condoms are not 100 percent effective, although using one properly does greatly lower your chances of contracting an STI.

Many guys (and women too!) do not like to use condoms and will come up with every excuse to go without one, having asked minimal questions of their partner around sexual history or birth control. The reason many people do not use condoms is that they don't like the feel and believe sex is more pleasurable without them. However, STIs and accidental pregnancies do not feel good, either. It is common for many men to deliver these lines, and if he continues to push the point, you need to question what level of respect he is giving your safety and what level of respect you have for yourself if you cross this boundary. If he is so willing to have unprotected sex with you, then it only increases the odds that he has had unprotected sex with others before you.

If you are losing the battle to his pleas or your own lustfulness, consider whether this person you are about to have unprotected sex with is worth contracting an STI for, some of which are lifelong, or if you are prepared to experience an accidental pregnancy with them. There is now the emergency contraceptive pill (also known as the morning-after pill), which can be used within 72 hours of unprotected sexual intercourse or if contraception failed (the condom broke), but this is still not completely effective in preventing pregnancies (approximately 85 percent) and does not stop the transmission of any STIs.

If you do find yourself in the position of having had unprotected sex outside a monogamous relationship, it's important not to feel judged but to instead take the correct course of action to minimize any further risk. See a doctor and consider if the emergency contraceptive pill is needed. You might also want to discuss options with your medical professional on how to keep yourself safer according to your individual sexual lifestyle.

Take a Walk on the Kinky Side

It's been so long since I've had sex I've forgotten who ties up whom.
—Joan Rivers

If there has been something on your mind that has intrigued you, this SBD time in your life is the perfect circumstance in which to explore it—I call this *sexploration*. With an official partner, the risks might be too high to get super-kinky; there is no turning back once you have crossed a boundary or experienced something that might have a negative backlash in the relationship.

You might have heard myths or stories of others' experiences that have added to the intrigue or taboo of a new sexual act— and that makes it all the more exciting! However, be prepared that when you finally realize a sexual fantasy, it might not be all that you imagined. A fantasy is sometimes better left a fantasy. Just ask yourself: do you want to explore sexual fantasies or urges because they are a real turn-on for you, or are they only turning you on because they feel somewhat out of bounds?

If you are going to explore something a little kinkier in the SBD world, here are a few tips that might assist you in doing so.

- Discuss your fantasies and what you find kinky.
- Establish trust through communication. This is vital, as you might not know how you will react or feel when you do experiment.
- Discuss boundaries. Having a safe or stop word or signals to exit an activity or location can be helpful.
- Test out your desired act using fantasy. Talk about whatever it is you want to explore during sex with that person to see how you both feel and react.

Exercise—Sexual Fantasies

It's good to work out what your sexual fantasies are and know the things you may possibly want to try. When you are put on the spot or in the moment, you might not be able to recall what they all are, so I suggest you start a list. Let's call this the *yes/no/maybe* list.

In three columns, you are going to write everything you would do (which can help when you are trying to think of sexual acts you are comfortable with), everything you wouldn't do (a reminder of your boundaries) and things you are open to considering. Make sure to explore why something is in the *maybe* column. Is it something you are not entirely comfortable with or have you just not found the right circumstance and situations to live it out?

Yes	No	Maybe

Are You Thinking with Your Brain or Your Vulva?

There is a growing trend among women to have sex not only when and with whom they please (a style that was historically more characteristic of men), but also with less consideration and an "I'll do what feels good" attitude. But we need to question with what organ we make these decisions—our vulva or our brain?

Every time I have the urge for chocolate, it doesn't mean that I should have it. It's something I choose to eat when my desire is strong and after much thought; I am fully aware of the consequences when I do. Just like with food, we need to find a balance when we make decisions around our sexuality. Sometimes our vulva does get the better of us and, just like the heart, it wants what it wants. But unlike our heads, it doesn't have the ability to factor in information surrounding the sexual act and possible consequences.

This doesn't mean that sex always has to be a calculated move, but our sexual urges should run through our cognitive minds before we make a move, just to ensure we are thinking them through to their conclusion.

How Does Porn Inform?

Erotica is using a feather; pornography is using the whole chicken.
—Isabel Allende

The *should* curse comes back into play when we talk about pornography. Pornography is a medium that gives us a lot of material to consider for our sexual lives, but we must remember that it is meant to entertain us and turn us on, not as an educational guide to be copied. For women who watch pornography, it's important to consider whether their sexual choices are *really* what they want or what they think they *should* want based on something they've seen in a pornographic film.

As pornography continues to get kinkier and kinkier, we need to remember that what we see in porn is *not reality*, no matter how normalized the acts may appear on screen. For example, where anal sex was once taboo and considered a specialty, it's now the norm in a lot of porn. That doesn't mean your feelings about having anal sex in real life have to change.

The shock value continues to rise: now that we live in a digital age, there is even virtual reality porn, where users can purchase a pair of goggles, looking through which gives them the sensation they are participating in a sexual encounter. Don't feel that you need to jump on these bandwagons if your inclination to comes from the porn stars you think you *should* find sexy. They're just actors. Pornography can be fun, empowering and pleasurable under the right circumstances, but challenge what part of our sexual behaviors are innate and which are due to the pressures that come from the material we take in.

Validation and Attention

In an SBD world where sex and appearances are given a lot of consideration, it can be tempting to start measuring your own self-worth by the sexual attention you receive. But the pursuit of confidence, attention or validation through sexual conquests (or even by flaunting sexuality) can have a serious downside.

As I mentioned earlier in the book during our discussion of confidence, when you are authentically confident, you don't need to validate yourself with sex or sexual attention as a form of accomplishment. If you lack that confidence, you will almost certainly begin accepting sexual offers and attention because you want to be liked and *not* because you have the sexual or romantic urge to do so.

If you are having sex just to be able to brag to your friends, you should question how good the sex really is, how it is really making you feel inside, and if your pleasure is coming more from the encounter itself or from the short-lived validation you receive from yourself or others for having that experience.

Having sex for validation can be a short-lived pleasure: the need of more sex for the next validation will be soon in sight. Good sex is about being present, connecting with someone and enjoying the moment—a high that will be more pleasurable and longer lasting than a romp just to prove something to yourself or others.

If you are flaunting your sexuality for attention, this might not be the true essence of who you are. It could actually be a wall you put up to hide who you really are and to block people from seeing the real you. In this case, you run the risk of people seeing you only as a sexual being, which will obscure your other positive attributes.

Sex as a Weapon

Some women are taught from a young age that they can use their sexuality to get things they want: to get a guy to like them, to keep a guy around, to manipulate or "train" him or maybe even to get a leg up (pun intended) in the workforce. It does happen and it can work. But using sex as a weapon is like using a loaded gun and can be just as dangerous. There are often unpredictable negative consequences and almost always a backlash down the line.

Let's take the example of using sex to get a guy to like you, or to fast-track a relationship. It might work for a while, but often game playing is met with more game playing. Just as you have used sex to get his interest, he might use sex to boost his ego, having accomplished the challenge you set for him. Just because he is having sex with you does not mean he likes you. Men want sex and will say what they need to in order to get it. You might think you are making a move in the direction of winning him over, but he may think he has won the sex lottery and nothing more. If all you want is sex and you don't care about the consequences, fine—but if you want something more and to feel respected and valued, sex isn't the way to do it.

Chapter 4

Cummunicating

I was dating this guy and we would spend all day
text messaging each other. He thought he could tell
that he liked me more because he actually spelled
the word "you" and I just put the letter "u."
—Kelly Osbourne

Because the lines are blurrier, relationships are more loosely defined and traditional rules don't seem to apply in the SBD world, it is even more crucial for guidelines to be discussed and agreed upon through effective communication.

When it comes to communication, men and women can be very different—it's sometimes as though we speak different languages altogether! However, there are ways for you to become more competent with it, even in sex and dating scenarios (which can be tricky). The key is, firstly, to get to know the person you are dealing with. To do this, really listen to them and ask questions. When you get a feel for who this person is, you can decide how they best hear (maybe they respond more to encouragement, maybe to personal stories, maybe to jokes). This will help you communicate to be heard and understood and decrease room for miscommunication.

Communication: The Key to Sexcess

Mind readers are few and far between, especially among men. If we could only tell our partners exactly what we wanted from them before sex, how much easier things would be! The trouble is that, especially in new situations, that communication might not be terribly comfortable or sexy. Making sexual demands without knowing where someone's boundaries or sexual tastes are runs the risk of turning them off. It's much easier to be open with someone when you know them enough to anticipate how they might react. If you're stuck between concern about being too forward with a new partner and the desire to enjoy your sexual experience, try starting with some subtle hints. Any great sexual experiences I've had have come from either frank conversation or subtle (or not-so-subtle and nonverbal) hints. We need good communication skills in order to enjoy our lives, dating and sexual experiences.

KISS Him

As you're doing all this communication in your SBD life, you'll undoubtedly run into the question of when to communicate what. If you need to have a deep and meaningful (D&M) conversation with a guy about the boundaries of your relationship, you may not want to do that on the way to a social event, for example. To determine when the time is right, I use the KISS principle: keep it simple, stupid! I've heard this slogan used in many situations, but I like to use it when communicating with men.

Be prepared to receive the KISS principle in return. Men are great with straightforward and honest answers. Don't take brief responses personally but just for what they are—the direct answer he thinks you are looking for. Be sure not to go analyzing his responses for a negative or hidden meaning—it's likely his response is simple and literal.

Never ask a man (or anyone) a question if you are trying to trick him into giving a certain answer or to see where his mind is. If you want to ask him something, ask him.

If you want to have a D&M, timing is important. Thank goodness you can often tell from a man's mannerisms when he is happy, sad, hungry or hangry or doesn't want to be bothered—just look. Timing can be everything and, if we are smart, we can use it to our advantage. If we want to be heard, don't try to compete with a football game or other passion. Keeping it simple in general, too, can help things run more smoothly.

How to Tell Him He's Bad in Bed (Nicely)

Communicating can be complex in general, but communicating dissatisfaction (especially about dating and sex) seems to be the most difficult thing of all, particularly when you are an SBD woman and possibly in a casual situation. I never look forward to giving out criticism because I hate the idea of incidentally hurting someone's feelings—they could very well be sensitive about their bedroom skills. Holding these issues inside, however, can cause resentment—and result in even more dissatisfaction.

Despite it not being easy or comfortable to ask for what you want (in the bedroom or in life) or having to give constructive criticism, we need to learn to sit with the feeling of embarrassment, discomfort or awkwardness it brings. If you don't, you'll be skirting the issues, likely arguing about nothing with no resolution, all because you have not confronted the real problem at hand. A little bit of awkwardness for a real solution and hopefully relief is a small price to pay.

The Sandwich Formula

Once you can deal with saying things that may be awkward, it's time to consider something I call the "sandwich" formula. This is not a guaranteed mathematical equation to solve every communication problem, but in the SBD world, which can be conversationally complex, it's a great tool. In a nutshell, you should place bad news, criticism or an awkward request between two bits of good news, to soften the blow.

Step 1: Start off with a compliment or say something you like about the person.

Step 2: Deliver the bad news, request or criticism swiftly and promptly, being careful what language you use so there is no room for misinterpretation.

Step 3: Follow with a quick compliment or another positive statement, different from the first.

Step 4: Because there is no point in just dumping bad news on someone and handing the problem over from your shoulders to theirs, you should now give the person hope and assure them that this problem will not be the end of whatever it is you are doing together: building a relationship, dating or casually hooking up.

Do your research and either suggest a few possible solutions to the issue or make a more specific request so they have something to work toward in the future.

Owning Your Emotions

In all conversations, it's a good idea to be aware of your emotions. Especially when communicating with someone whom you're involved with romantically or sexually, and therefore feel some emotion toward, it is a great exercise to think about how your emotions may be impacting—or hijacking—your communication.

For example, you may get mad because someone you went on a few dates with has seemingly vanished or ghosted you. You may feel ashamed, mad and wounded, but before you pick up the phone, fire off a text or post on social media, really examine the source of your feelings and consider the good (or harm) that a hasty action might do.

Is there some programming you learned as a child that triggers you to feel ashamed, abandoned or like you must have done something to deserve bad treatment? Because if you really think about it, it doesn't need to feel like such a deep wound that someone just showed you clearly they are not a kind or thoughtful person. You don't need to take that—or many other things that happen in the SBD world—too personally. It's never about you, anyway; it's about who that person is and how they treat people. Let go of any old programming and tell yourself, "I am worthy of kindness and respect" and "I am lovable just the way I am right now." These validating (and very true!) statements can help you reprogram old beliefs that are no longer serving you. They may help you be less reactive to less-than-ideal situations in front of you that ultimately aren't worth your time.

Another important communication rule is to make sure you own your own emotions. This means not starting emotional sentences with the word *you*. Instead of "you make me feel unattractive because you never give me attention or touch me in public," try, "I feel unattractive because you don't touch me in public and I feel you might be ashamed to be out with me." This approach makes it clear it's not his fault the way you feel (even though you might feel like it is) and that there is something he can do to help change the way you feel. Accusatory statements can cause many people (not just men) to shut down and become defensive.

It's common that a simple expression of displeasure about something can be interpreted as a nag by a romantic or sexual partner. Actually, asking him for something or to do something, even just once, could be perceived as a nag. To combat this unfair misinterpretation, use positive statements and reinforcement as an alternative to complaining. For example, instead of "Why don't you ever reply to my text messages?" or "Why don't you ever stay the night after we have sex?" try "I really love hearing from you over text—it puts a smile on my face" or "I really love it when you stay the night after we have sex." Men respond better to feeling as though they have done the right thing, instead of being scolded for something they are not doing or doing wrong. Like the saying goes, you catch more flies with honey than with vinegar. You can also try doubling down on this verbal positive reinforcement with a seductive glance or touch—this will help create even more of a positive association between the action he took and the pleasurable sensation of your response.

Nonverbal Communication

Words are a wonderful form of communication, but
they will never replace kisses and punches.
—Ashleigh Brilliant

We have known for many years that much of our communication is nonverbal. According to the psychologist Albert Mehrabian (who is well-known for his work on the relative importance of verbal and non-verbal messages), only about 7 percent of all communication is verbal, 38 percent is vocal, and 55 percent is visual (for example, body language and facial expressions). Considering men might not be listening to many words or complex questions, nonverbal communication can be a great way to get your message across. If you want to discuss something important and grab his attention, look him in the eyes (a man's primary sense is visual), turn your body toward him without your arms crossed (arms crossed can often display a negative body image or closed position) and touch him somewhere—on the arm, shoulder or leg. Touch can be a very powerful way to help someone trust you and what you are about to say, which often elicits a positive response. Combine that with the fact that touching him might even turn him on and you have one powerful communication tool in your hands—literally.

In exploring the world of nonverbal communication with men, it's vital to look at reinforcement to reward the good stuff you want him to continue to do. If the current man in your life does something great for you, rewarding him is easy. Humans love to be touched and we feel positive sensations when someone touches us—this is why touch feels like a reward. Give him a kiss, grab him by the arm passionately, give him a hug: these are all ways to positively reinforce someone's actions. You can go more extreme with your rewards, too (wink, wink), but if you reward him with anything sexual, make sure you don't get into the habit of *only* having sex when he has done something right. Sex is about connection and pleasure, not to be used as a bargaining chip.

When something is not right or there is a negative interaction that upsets someone, I think the tendency to want to "switch off" is only natural, but you need to be careful that you don't use this as a form of communication in and of itself. No one wants to be one of those women who, when asked if anything is wrong, replies, "Nothing; I'm fine," while turning away in a huff in the hope that he will pick up on her negative body language and instantly become a mind reader. This behavior is not easy to read. Remember the KISS principle? Well, this is anything but simple. If he takes you at your word, he's screwed (and this time not literally); if he doesn't, then it's a battle of mind reading to guess why you're not actually "fine." Don't make life more difficult by playing these confusing mind games.

If a man asks you what is wrong, tell him. Keep it short and don't make it too complicated. Strengthen your point by making sure your actions match your words—if you are going to scold him for something he has done wrong or for crossing a boundary, don't then go and stay the night or even engage in sexual activity with him if things haven't been resolved.

Silence Is Golden

Silence can be the key to getting a man to express his thoughts or fill in the gaps when you are having a conversation. For many women, when they are just getting to know a new male acquaintance, nerves can kick in and the fear of awkward silence makes motormouth take control. Give him a chance to talk. Don't you want to get to know a bit about him, too? Try calming down, pausing between your hilarious and entertaining stories and just looking at him calmly, giving him the opportunity and permission to have a say.

Wait, What?

If you do suspect that there has been miscommunication in a conversation with a romantic or sexual partner, or you just don't get what he is trying to say, clarify and paraphrase. If you were in a classroom and didn't understand something the teacher was saying, you would ask, so make sure to ask for clarification on anything that is confusing. Miscommunication is more common than we'd like, especially in the SBD world, where standards are a bit different, but following up with him to ensure you understood correctly will give you the chance to confirm you are on the same page.

Chapter 5

Where Did All the Men Go?

While creating men, God promised women that a
good and ideal man would be found in all the corners
of the world, then He made the earth round.
—Unknown

In our modern world, where it seems we have every tool at our fingertips to meet Mr. Right and Mr. Right Now, why are we left scratching our heads, wondering where all the good guys are and where we can meet them? It's as though the many dating options and avenues available and the quick, superficial level at which it's common to date are distracting us from the fact that there are great men all around us. We are blinded by distractions!

Matchmaker, Matchmaker, Make Me a Match

Sometimes we are so busy (and a bit self-absorbed) that we don't spend enough time setting up our friends. Social matchmaking can be a great way to connect friends from our networks with people from our wider social pool.

We may not even be aware of who is single in our lives. Have you asked your chiropractor or the girl who does your facial lately about their relationship status? (It might be a good idea to clarify why you are asking so you don't send out the wrong message!) This is not just about finding you a date, but finding dates for other people in your life, too. Think of this as dating karma. Don't just introduce two people because they are both single; take the time to see if there is something these people have in common and a reason they might connect. I have had so many attempts in the past by people to set me up with men just because they were single and Jewish. That was the only reason for the introduction. But single and Jewish doesn't ensure a good conversation, things in common or him not being a complete loser.

For the SBD woman who is keen to be set up: your friends, colleagues, hot neighbors, brother, cousins and anyone else in your life can be great resources to ask. It might never have crossed their minds to think of making an introduction for you. This is a way you can access men with some of the filtering processes done for you, especially if you are introduced by someone you trust and who understands you.

Some people do take offense when a suggestion is made about setting them up, as though the question implies they are unable to find a date for themselves, or are so desperate they need help. Your friends might not be matchmaking you because they don't want to offend you, so make your request nice and clear. Ask and you shall receive.

Some people are scared of looking desperate when asking to be set up. I sympathize with this because it took me quite some time to do. But if it casually comes up in conversation— if they mention in passing that a friend of theirs is dating some great girl or you are talking about dating in general—why not ask? Sometimes people need a little nudge to think outside of their own lives and start considering who is there in their social network.

I believe in social matchmaking. I proudly have two marriages, a long-term relationship and two babies as a result of my romantic meddling with friends, and hopefully it doesn't stop there.

I have also been successfully matched. When I did finally give in to a friend's request to set me up with a guy she insisted I would be good with, I met Peter. There was a certain level of ease because I trusted the person who had set us up and knew he wouldn't be a creep or player. We dated for a bit and I enjoyed his company, but in the end, there was just no spark. Friends might be able to pick you a nice guy, but they can't be certain of chemistry. If you are hesitant but trust your friend, just say yes. You don't have to marry the guy, just go and enjoy a nice dinner date with a bit more ease.

Online and App Dating

Dating online and on apps is now the norm and often feels as though it is overtaking meeting people in real life. The Pew Research Center found that use of online dating sites or mobile dating apps by young adults has nearly tripled since 2013. Today, nearly half the public knows someone who uses online dating or who has met a spouse or partner through online dating. When you go out into the night's meat market scene, it's hard to know who people really are or what they want. When you go online or use an app, you can be honest about exactly the type of person you want to meet and what you want from them. There is an online dating site and app for every different religion, age bracket, profession, sexual orientation or even STI status that you might share with someone to help narrow your search.

However, for all its helpfulness, the online dating world has so accelerated the process of meeting someone that it has in turn made us distracted and disposable. Instead of reading through profiles, a quick finger swipe left or right and a swift judgment of whether someone's photos are hot or not (or just plain creepy) are all that's needed.

If you are keen to date multiple people, these are the perfect platforms to do so. Meeting and dating multiple men in the physical world can be difficult and time-consuming, so if you do want a few options at once but still have to manage a life and a career, then finding Mr. Right Now online might just be the way to go. This can make an SBD woman's life action-packed— but it can also make a woman easily replaceable. Just as we are able to swipe to the next guy after a brief judgment, so can men do the same to us.

Some online sites and apps also allow us to easily find and date members of the same sex with the simple option to switch between genders or look for both at one time. At any rate, make sure to be honest with who you are and why you are on a given app or site. We must remember that there are always someone else's feelings on the other side of your phone and no one wants to be treated like a lab experiment.

Online Dating Downers

You've probably heard the term *catfishing* with respect to online dating. If I met someone in person who was not quite the

Adonis his online photos led me to believe, but whom I felt a connection with or who made me smile, the likelihood is that I would go out with him and get to know him. Personality can and should mean more than looks (if you have started to master the art of mature dating instead of just superficial dating), so as long as there is something that first intrigues me about them and leaves me wanting to know more, I'll see it through.

We also can't see non-superficial qualities online, which is another big drawback of dating in the digital age. I used to study and analyze every little thing in an online profile—small details in a person's description and photos—which is also not conducive to keeping an open mind.

We tend to rely on online dating so much that old-fashioned dating etiquette and ways of meeting people in person seem less and less common. If you were a guy before the internet and you jumped into an elevator with a good-looking girl, you might have started up a conversation with her. Nowadays, I think guys see a good-looking girl and unless she is the woman of their dreams, they are unlikely to bother speaking to her, as there are plenty of hot women waiting for them online or a text away—or because they are shy and not confident enough to talk to a stranger, as they haven't had much practice (also because of the prevalence of meeting people online). It's almost so easy to date online that the effort to do it in person no longer seems worth it. Too many online options are killing the motivation to work on our interpersonal skills.

This works both ways: women also are not starting up conversations or—thanks to having their heads down in their phones or because of their other dismissive behaviors—not even appearing to be open to a man starting a conversation with them. I've heard many women complain about a lack of male attention, but maybe we women are also sending off unfriendly signals. Are women subconsciously silencing advances IRL (in real life) because they feel they don't have to worry about being open, flirty and polite because they are dating online? As with many things in the digital age, it's a balancing act. You might be learning more technical skills, but don't forget about your interpersonal and in-person flirting skills in the process.

For many people, seeing a match on their dating app or knowing someone is interested in their profile is the main reward they're after and a relationship never progresses beyond that. That may seem silly for how much time online dating can take, but it's true. Sometimes no conversations are even had or a simple "hi" or "hello" is the extent of the interaction. If you have noticed that you have many matches on apps but not the same number of conversations started, keep this in mind: it's not you and there is nothing wrong with you! Many men just use these apps as an ego boost or a game to see how many matches they can win—they might not be too focused on an outcome from it. They may even be in a relationship and just on an app to sniff out the BBD (bigger, better deal). It's not right, but again, it's true. Challenge yourself to see if you might be doing the same. Also consider that many men don't seem to get how to start an active conversation online. If you like the look of him, try some questions that require answers.

How to Make Better Matches Online

Just as you would not go to meet someone at certain bars and clubs that might say something about your personality and the personality of those you might meet, so too will the places you choose to date online reflect something about you.

It's great to be able to have at least something in common when you begin dating—it's a good starting-off point. Online profiles allow you to set boundaries for deal-breakers. If you are career-driven and also looking for someone who is ambitious and that is a deal-breaker for you, then just being on a site for young professionals will set up that boundary. Choose the one thing that is important to you when it comes to dating: a hobby, religion or even the type of relationship you want to engage in. That will act as a filter for your matches. In some cases, being in the SBD world might mean you're on a site that you wouldn't otherwise join were you looking for a relationship or someone with whom to go out on a date.

Online Dating Tips

- Don't give away too much in your profile. This is not a place for your life story (and it may not be read, anyway).
- Choose photos where you look happy and include one natural shot, where you are wearing the amount of makeup you wear on a regular day (not for a special occasion).
- Avoid photos with too many other people, as it might get confusing as to which person you are and who the others are, too.
- Use your photos to describe yourself. If you like dogs, include a photo with your dog. If you are active, choose a photo on a hike or playing a sport. If you love traveling, choose snaps from your latest vacation. A picture is worth a thousand words.

- When filtering through profiles, keep an open mind and remember the goal is to date maturely, not superficially. Try to find something that intrigues you instead of something that just attracts you physically.

- Don't be afraid to say hi to a guy first. There are so many people in the online dating world, sometimes you need to be a bit forward. Guys can not only be inundated with options, but they can be shy, too. If you don't start chatting to them, how will you know if they have wit and charm? Ask a question about his profile or say something that elicits a response to keep the conversation going, but still give him room to pursue you.

- If you can sense he is a little shy or if he has mentioned catching up but hasn't set a date, suggest some times you might be free or activities you're keen to engage in.

- Know when to back off. If you are messaging away with little or no response, perhaps you should take the hint. In the online world, rejection will only hurt momentarily, until you get distracted by life or move on to the next guy (which could be within minutes).

- Master the art of good online banter. This should not be your life story—keep the conversation light—but it should be interesting enough that he can get an idea of what you're all about (and so that you'll stand out from the crowd). Again, ask questions and give statements that require responses to keep the conversation going.

- Social media. It's a good idea to use social media to cross-check that at least his name and appearance match up with his dating profile, but beware of learning everything about him straight away. Social media can also represent a false reality, so don't count on it to be accurate.

Use it just to make sure he isn't an ax murderer, then leave everything else for your face-to-face conversation.

- When you match with someone who has mutual friends on Facebook, think twice before ringing them up to investigate him. I would advise that you meet your date before getting the word on him from his friends, so you are able to make up your own mind rather than be influenced by someone else's.
- Consider if you have too many mutual friends. If you are only looking for some casual fun, then being in the same social circle can backfire. We've all heard the advice, "Don't shit where you eat."
- Be careful that attention from online dates does not become your self-esteem crutch.
- Just because you match with someone and start chatting with them does not mean you are in a pre-relationship.
- If you do end up dating someone you met online, always assume that they are seeing multiple people. This will help keep you realistic and remain on the market, too.
- Don't take too long to reply to messages, either out of laziness or game playing. There might be lots of other people vying for his attention.
- Don't bother being offended when men send you unsolicited sexual messages or images (cock shots, dick pics and requests for photos of you). Don't waste your energy trying to correct or scold them; just block and move on if it bothers you.
- Include on your profile why you are on a given app or site. The purpose of some dating apps can be quite broad and confusing and you don't want to find yourself offended mid-drink when your date expects an invitation back home.

- Consider how much is too much when dating from online apps. Although it may be wise to have a few men in the mix, a different date every night of the week can be overwhelming!

When Online Dating Meets the Real World

The online world can help us meet new people, but your life online can be very different from your life in person, and at some stage, the two will intersect.

Don't spend too much time talking with someone online or on the phone. The longer you spend with someone purely online, the more you might start to make decisions about their personality, the scenario and maybe even the fairytale inside your head. Put down the phone and make plans to meet in person.

Do a background check. This might be a quick Google search, an Instagram search or by swapping phone numbers and some photos or texts. A Google search has always been my best weapon: I once avoided dating a convicted drug smuggler and a married man all because I JGFGI'ed (Just Go Fucking Google It) them. If you search for him online, only do it for safety; try not to judge him too superficially on what you see. You need to ensure that he is who he says he is and have a chance to suss out anything that might feel wrong using your gut instincts. If things don't add up, proceed with caution or continue on to the next profile.

With first encounters, try somewhere casual with lots of people around. Think of this as testing the waters to see if you then want to go out on a proper date (or even more). It's as though you met him at a bar but knew he was going to be there. I wish I could tell you internet dating was 100 percent safe, but it isn't. Since you are technically meeting up with a stranger (whom you may think you know after a few chats), it's also good to let a friend know where you are going and whom you are with.

Distraction Dating at Its Best (Or Worst)

Online dating has made dating multiple people the norm. When you meet someone online, you know that they are probably not only seeing other people while they are dating you, but actively looking for others as well. This technology can be great for meeting new people, but if you want more, or even just want some of his distracted attention, you could find a battle on your hands. This works both ways: you might not be able to focus on him or get to know him more intimately because you are distracted, thinking of the next night's date or the next right swipe.

If we were to attempt to date multiple people the old-fashioned way—in person—it would take some serious time and effort, so the number of people we were dating probably couldn't get too outrageously high. With online dating, however, the number of people we might be talking to or seeing, and the number of people whom *they* might be talking to or seeing, could be nearly endless. With this in mind, it would be easy to be picky and reject someone for the most minute or bizarre reasons—we can just swipe to someone new. We must not fall into that trap!

There is a balance between knowing what you want and

being too picky, and, while a great way to meet new people, dating apps allow us to date from a judgmental and superficial point of view. If we are not careful, this will cause us to undoubtedly miss out on lots of Mr. Right Nows, if not some Mr. Rights (if that's what you're looking for).

Stigmas of App and Online Dating

Just as it can be difficult to tell what the purpose of a given dating app is, it's also tricky to articulate what it means to have an online dating presence at all. For varying reasons, some apps—or online dating in general—have been stigmatized. Some apps are seen as purely "hookup apps," for example, and future dates could judge you for having used them.

Dating apps can also have the stigma of careless behavior. Rejection online can make you feel down, and it can be amplified if you feel like someone rejected you without even getting to know you. This is the part of online dating that can wreak havoc on us if we are not in a strong and confident place. If you are feeling vulnerable or a bit sensitive or if your headspace is not entirely positive, you may be more inclined to focus on the negative aspects of online dating (rejection) rather than the perks (meeting new people), and it may be time to take a break from digital dating—or even go on a man ban.

Empowering the Modern Woman

Online dating has helped pave the way for sexual and dating liberation for women. When it comes to the online and app world, there is a certain level of anonymity for a woman seeking fun: she is able to discreetly and easily let someone know that she is keen to chat (or something more) from the click of her phone without even leaving her house and with a minimal risk of judgment by others. If she likes a person and they don't like her back, they might never know that she attempted to put out the signal, saving her any embarrassment or feelings of awkwardness.

Dating apps are full of fun, sexual experiences, unwanted (and maybe some wanted) dick pics and distractions, but they are also a great reminder to SBD women that there are singles out there. A friend once told me that although no dates resulted from her being online and she was just chatting with a few guys, simply being on the app changed her attitude—it made her realize how many single men were out there! Instead of walking around thinking all the men around her were taken, she became more open-minded. If there were all these available guys on apps, then some of the men around her might be single, too.

Meeting Men on Social Media

I'm a big believer that social media is for social media and dating sites and apps are for meeting, dating and hooking up. But there are always exceptions to the rule. I know one girl who is married to a man who started sending her DMs on Twitter. There is one major problem with using social media to date people online—the messages can get confusing and your romantic or sexual intentions can be lost. He might think you are just keeping in touch or being social when you send your friend request, unaware that you want more. At least with dating sites and apps, your intentions are clear; with social media, to get the message across you may need to be all the more forward.

You might also run the risk of giving TMI (too much information). Consider what your online photos and content might say about you and how a guy might perceive them. How many elevator selfies and duck face poses have you posted? If he asks to add you on Facebook as a way to stay in touch (if you have read the signals right), offer him your phone number instead.

When a stranger requests your friendship online, proceed with caution. You don't know his intention, how he found you or what conclusion he is making about you from your social media account, which is much like your private, online world. Would he find the same amount of information about you from a dating app as he would from your Facebook or Instagram page?

Singles Events

Singles events are a bit less common these days and they do have a certain element of awkwardness, but they are also good practice to switch off your phone and be present. Dating is not always comfortable, but like anything, with more practice and experience it becomes easier.

The good news is that intentions at singles events are clear—everyone is single and ready to mingle. With these events, you can get away with questions that are much more direct, getting to what you want out of a partner (and even out of life) more efficiently. You are trying to discover compatibility in a short period of time. These events can be anything from speed dating to a group singles dinner put on by a friend. The important thing to note here is to have an open mind and go with the flow. If you get an invite to attend something single-esque, why not give it a go? What do you have to lose except time? You could gain confidence and practice your dating skills.

Flirting with Finesse: The Holy Grail of Dating

If old-fashioned dating skills are dwindling because of technology, we might need to send men an encouraging push. Men can be very wary of rejection and, as we've discussed, occasionally intimidated by the modern alpha female, so it's a good idea to send more of those flirtatious signals that tell a guy it's okay to talk to us and even try to pick us up. I'm finding it so common that women think they are being rejected, but in actuality, the guy has pulled away a bit because he is not getting clear-enough signals from her and thinks he is being rejected himself!

The biggest problem with flirting is that there are no rules, laws or boundaries to what flirting might look like; growing up, we are not taught how to flirt—everyone learns it from somewhere different so it often looks very different. Some behaviors are subconscious and others are expressed with a bit more force. There is an obvious distinction between general flirting and flirting with the intent to pick up someone. Flirting can be a single woman's best tool—a balancing act between remaining the woman who is pursued by a man and also letting a man know she wants to be pursued. Many women are too embarrassed to just go up to a guy they think is hot and say "hi"—they want to be chased. Flirting can be a way of encouraging an introduction and getting the attention of a man for the right reasons.

Think of flirting like app dating—swiping left and right in real life. A closed body posture, turning the other way or answering with short sentences might tell a guy you are not interested and to leave you alone (swipe left). But there are a multitude of things you can do to tell him you want him to talk to you or that you'd be inviting of his advances (swipe right).

In the beginning of a dating scene, when a woman and a man are standing in a bar, club or restaurant, the man will be more likely to approach a woman or make the first move if he thinks she is into him, as it eliminates his potential for rejection. It's common in our social modern culture to meet new friends of the opposite sex out and about; flirting is one way you can demonstrate the difference in your intentions between wanting to be mates with someone and hoping for more.

If you are at a bar or standing near someone at the gym and want to send the message "I want you to come and say 'hi' to me," there are various things you can do to assist your natural flirtatious behaviors. Many of these tips may sound outdated to the modern woman, but trust me, they have stood the test of time *because they work.*

- Eye contact. Show him that you want to talk with him using your eyes. You might need to look at him—then look away—then look back again a few times to drum in that message.
- Smiling and laughing. Happy people are sexy people. People always want to talk to happy people. There is a reason that we all tend to giggle more easily when we are flirting—laughing shows we are having fun—but be self-aware; too much unwarranted laughter can seem fake.

- Posture. Posture can say a lot about a person. Does yours say that you are confident or shy and insecure?
- Touch. Touch is a great way to let him know you want more than just banter or friendship. Touching him on the arm, thigh or lower back does that nicely.
- Physical distance. If you are in a bar or a crowded space and you start to make eye contact (or have what feels like eye sex) with a guy on the other side of the room and want to up the odds, move! It makes life a little easier. Not only are you sending a loud and clear message, you are making the encounter more likely by making logistics easier for him.
- Appearance. Flirting is not always about the direct invitations we give to someone but the indirect messages we send by how we present ourselves. Every time you step out of the house, take a moment to consider what message your appearance might send about you. It doesn't mean life should be a constant catwalk, but let's take the example of workout gear: I love being in my workout gear but still manage to display that I'm a confident woman because I choose colorful pieces, not baggy, torn ones.

Creepy, Cool. Potato, Potahto.

What happens when there is a guy floating around in your life whom you're keen on but you haven't quite managed to get his attention? Be in the right place at the right time. Now, this is where there is a thin line between flirting and stalking. I'm not suggesting you stalk him—just place yourself in areas where you know he might hang out or choose to meet friends at a bar you know he frequents. If you run into him, you'll be able to flaunt your best and flirt it up!

It's important to note there is a difference between picking men up with flirtatious invitations and throwing yourself at them. Flirting is about sending the right signals, not necessarily making the first (obvious) move. If you do make the first move, why not let him do some of the work, too?

Another key to flirting is knowing when to back off if you are not sure he's into you. Walk away either physically or metaphorically, not to "be mean, keep 'em keen," but to test out his level of interest. Don't fear if he does not follow—you will not click with every guy out there. If a guy isn't into you, it doesn't mean that there is something wrong with you, but that you might not be the right fit together or that he has something going on in his life that is taking him off the market. Have the confidence to back off and to be okay if he doesn't come after you when you do. These challenging situations are why being a confident dater is paramount.

The Bar and Nightclub Scene

If you just want to find someone with good looks or who is a good dancer, it's easy at a nightclub, but anything more can seem impossible to identify in that environment. Conversations tend to be briefer and less in depth, and the lighting is dark. That can be great for a hookup, but if you want to swap numbers with eligible men to date, I suggest heading to a high-end bar with female friends only (but not too many), where the cocktails are still flowing but the vibe is conducive to chatting and flirting. I hate to encourage alcohol, but if you are very shy, one or two drinks can be helpful. Just enough to lower your inhibitions to help you talk to that guy, but not so much that everyone becomes attractive (except for drunken you, who is slurring and trying to stay upright). Personally, I like to remember the rule that "one is fun." If you are feeling pressured to drink but don't want to, my best secret is always to order soda water in a champagne glass or in a small glass with a wedge of lime. Champagne or vodka and soda? Who's to know?

It is safe to assume that there are a number of people at any bar who are single and looking to mingle. If not, maybe they have friends who are single and looking to mingle. Don't be scared to start up conversations and enjoy making new friends (or more than friends). Ask how his night is going or what cocktail he's drinking or even drop a compliment on his outfit—and don't forget to smile and give a cheeky grin. The goal at a bar is not only to flirt by sending out nonverbal signals, but also to find an excuse to start talking with him. This is where phones need to be put away! Even if you are on your own or waiting for a friend to arrive, put your phone in your bag and look up at who's around. A woman staring down at her phone and text messaging doesn't exactly appear to be open to someone starting a conversation with her. Don't be scared to take yourself out of your comfort zone. What's the worst that can happen—you could feel embarrassed? It's just another night at a bar, and no one but you will remember.

If you do meet a man at a bar or nightclub, don't be surprised if, in the outside world, he is not exactly the man of your dreams. Things tend to look different once the sun is shining. But you may meet a nice guy out on the town, have fun and swap numbers or even go to bed together, and if you do, make sure you take the next meeting as the proper first date. He could be your next Mr. Right Now.

How to Talk to Men

When trying to talk to members of the opposite sex outside of the bar and nightclub environment, *almost any* excuse to start up a conversation will do. Be aware of your surroundings for clues as to an icebreaker or come up with creative excuses. Sometimes the more creative, the more memorable.

Once again, it's vital that the phone is dissed! For just one week, I suggest you try going around town talking to the strangers in your life. Maybe ask the guy in the lift in your building if he had a good weekend or make a comment about the weather. Ask the hottie lifting weights at the gym how to use a particular piece of equipment (even if you already know). Start up a conversation with the guy next to you in line for his morning coffee. I'm not suggesting that these are going to be the men you end up going on a date with or sleeping with, but you need to start somewhere when it comes to learning how to make conversation with strangers. If you start here, I promise the rest will become easier and you will begin to lose some of the fear around talking to people you don't know. Practice might not quite make perfect, but it will certainly give you more confidence.

Here is the conversation-starter formula I follow: First, make a statement. Second, ask a question (that requires a response) that relates to the topic you made a statement about. Doing this in a super-friendly and open manner puts the other person at ease and will make them want to talk back with you.

Here are a few ideas for general conversation topics that may help:

- Something that is on him. This could be something he is wearing, a dog he's walking or something he is carrying (like a drink he has in his hand). This thing could be a clue as to where he is going (e.g., board shorts may mean a trip to the beach). I once got talking to a guy because it seemed we were nearly wearing matching outfits and we both had a giggle. Be observant so that you can talk about something that is relevant. Perhaps you ask which way you should go to avoid traffic or what you should buy your brother for his birthday because he looks like a man with good style.

- Something that is going on around you or the setting you are in. If you can't think of anything else, the weather is always a safe topic (but can also be a bit mundane). Are you lining up for a coffee or busy at the gym? These are things you are able to comment on and ask his opinion or pose a question. I once got talking to a guy in an adult shop about what he was purchasing after my friend and I had gone in for a little shop after cocktails one night. It was a great way to humorously get the conversation going; however, I should have stopped to first consider whom he was purchasing the nipple clamps for! Alert, married man!

- Jokes. If there is a clear opportunity to make a funny or sarcastic comment, go for it! Humor is a sure way to get the ball rolling.

When you make any of these statements and questions, don't forget to look him in the eyes and smile. This is your way of clearly letting him know you want him to talk to you and that you are a fun and confident person to talk to.

Run from Your Rut

It's easy to get stuck in a rut when it comes to meeting *new* men in your life. You might be going to the same gym, the same bar and the same coffee house you always have, which means it's likely you'll see the same people you always have. If this sounds familiar to you, it's time to spice up your everyday life. Doing something different can not only stimulate our brains and make us happy, but it can also put us in contact with brand-new people whom we might have something in common with.

Exercise—Discovering Where to Meet Men

If you are stuck in a bit of a dating rut or just eager to discover new places to meet more eligible men, it can help to explore your own world and list places you should start attending. Writing these down will set your intention to make a visit.

First, write down all the usual places that you go (work, public transport, coffee shop, gym, bar, etc.)—then think about what the men are like at those places. Have you met any men there or even spoken to any? (Keep in mind you might need to go back to these same places with your new open mind and flirting abilities.)

Second, write down places that you have either always wanted to go or that could be an alternative to those you currently attend but are feeling get you nowhere in terms of dates and men. Is there a new gym you have heard about that has lots of cute singles? You may have to shop around a bit. Is it time to change your local bar? A new environment might help you get out of your rut and open you to new possibilities.

Usual Place You Go	New Alternative

"Hello, Would You Like to Have Sex with Me?"

A modern SBD woman is, by all means, allowed to pick up men, even if it's just for casual sex. If you are shy about this, again I urge you to consider what the worst that could happen is—he could say no? Even then you'd gain some experience for the next time.

I do, however, think that the way to ask for casual sex is very dependent on a given situation. He might be shy and need you to make the first move; you might be feeling really keen and confident; or you might just be in one of those moods where you want sex and are attracted to him and don't care how it happens. Even when casual sex is all that's on the table, there is still the male/female dynamic to contend with—some men love a bit of a challenge; others are turned on by a confident woman who can directly pick them up. How will you know which one he is?

If you do want to give picking up a man a go, test the waters first and see how he responds. Go up and start a conversation flirtatiously, but maybe refrain from asking for his number or throwing in "Wanna come back to mine?" unless you are receiving positive signals back from him. Even if it is just casual sex you are after, there is no need to be crass (even though some men might respond to it). You can want sex and still maintain elegance and class. Try to cheekily suggest a change of setting to somewhere you know sex will be a possibility—a drink back at yours or a movie night on the couch, for example. You could ask to see the view from his apartment or invite him to check out your home decorating skills. If all else fails, a simple request to go somewhere more private usually does the trick.

Dating Tips from a Male Social Coach

James Maclane, a social coach from Australia, advises that we assess the size of the group we, as women, go out in—two is too few, as it can be awkward for a man to try to talk to one girl who is concerned about leaving her friend out, and a large group can be intimidating for a guy to approach if all the girls are huddled in the corner of a bar or club.

Maclane's next advice is to ditch the "too cool for school" face. Women who appear to think they are above everyone else are turnoffs; men want someone sweet, feminine and a bit vulnerable. Maclane suggests we take notes from Marilyn Monroe for two particular reasons: Marilyn managed to come off as confident but also vulnerable and in need of male protection. At the same time, she was flirtatious and seemed sexually available. According to Maclane, "If you put those two factors together, it's like crack to a man's brain."

Maclane warns women to be careful of the "be mean, keep 'em keen" tactic. Testing men too much or pushing them away (even to get them running back) can scare them off.

When putting all this advice into action, there is one more thing to consider—a few key male personality types. This is not a matter of labeling but understanding some dating dynamics with men in order to make informed decisions about how involved you want to get.

Women with low self-esteem love bad boys. Women who have work to do love bad boys. Women who love themselves love good men.
—Tracy McMillan

Stranger Danger!
Personality Types to Watch Out For

Mr. Fuck It, I Want It

There comes a time in every woman's life when only one phrase applies: "Fuck it, I want it." This is the sexual equivalent of giving in to a craving for chocolate when you are trying to cut back on sweets. All logic goes out the window and you do it anyway, just because you want to.

The only advice I can give when you run into Mr. Fuck It, I Want It is that he could be the riskiest fun you might have; there is always a consequence to the Fuck It way of life. Sometimes we simply want what we want—just make sure you consider all the possible repercussions. Also, ensure you have a great support system in place to catch you if things end badly.

Mr. Married

We are often attracted to what we can't have or what is out of bounds. Mr. Married can be charming and affectionate and knows exactly how to treat a woman he is pursuing.

Some women love playing the mistress or being adored and appreciated by a man who may be starved of sexy affection at home. Some women fall for Mr. Married only for a bit of lavish fun, but others get stuck with the promise of him leaving his wife.

Mr. Married may also flirt with crossing the line of physical infidelity without actually doing it—sending saucy texts and maybe even sneaking away from his wife to send you naked photos. A good rule of thumb is that if something has to be hidden, you need to consider if it's appropriate behavior.

Mr. Insecure

Many men use exterior things to increase their sense of self-worth: cars, appearance, money, drugs, possessions and, of course, women. Men with issues around insecurity can be a big problem and insecurity is not always easy to spot. Especially if a woman is younger or inexperienced in the dating world or even suffering from self-doubt herself, Mr. Insecure might appear to be exactly what she needs—always wanting her and needing to make sure she is his. But that need might not necessarily be because Mr. Insecure actually needs or wants that woman, but because he needs that woman to want him in return, to give him security. Winning you makes him feel like he has accomplished something. Dating a Mr. Insecure can be a toxic spiral out of control because no amount of attention can fulfill him.

There might be various perks to dating Mr. Insecure that can make it fun for a while, but an insecure man is likely one who will want to control you, too. Instead of getting to know you and what you want, he is more likely to buy your love and affection with either monetary possessions or with the attention he gives you. Although he may make you feel like you are on top of the world, he won't do it with real love but with obsessive tendencies and the hidden agenda that his attention will keep you coming back for more and you'll begin to need him as much as he needs you. If you are dating or sleeping with an insecure man, you may find the time you spend with him is full of tricks and tactics to get you to boost his ego. A secure man will want to make you feel good because he cares about you, not because he feels like it will lock you in or it is a trick to keep you in his grip to make him feel good about himself.

The checklist below is long because there is a lot to look out for with Mr. Insecure. At a more serious level, Mr. Insecure can be damaging not only to a woman's self-esteem but also to her physical safety. As a side note, many men you will meet may tick some things off this list (we all suffer from some form of insecurity), but the point at which a man goes from having normal insecurities to dangerous ones is something you will have to decide for yourself. Here are some behaviors rooted in insecurity that can be signs of trouble:

- Overly concerned and consumed with his own appearance. There is a line between wanting to look our best and using our outside appearance to mask inside insecurities. Is his gym-going lifestyle to keep healthy and fit, or to obsess over every bit of fat and muscle (or lack thereof)?

- A short amount of time between girlfriends. Insecure men move on very quickly because they always need a woman by their side.

- Dating beautiful, shy or young women. Insecure men often use beautiful women as an ego boost for their lack of confidence. Insecure men also tend to date shy and younger women, as their inexperience in the dating world can sometimes mean they are easier to control.

- A reputation as a player. Mr. Insecure often boosts his ego by using women and then moving on to the next.

- Talking badly about ex-girlfriends. According to Mr. Insecure, all his ex-girlfriends will be psychos or weirdos, because of course they would have to have something mentally wrong with them if they are no longer with him.

- Cheated in the past. There are so many reasons that a man might cheat, but a very common one is that he is looking to stroke his ego (in addition to his member). Often one woman is not enough.

- Trying to win you over with superficial things. Fancy restaurants, picking you up in expensive cars and maybe even some presents can be nice from time to time, but there is a line. Handbags are always a great giveaway. When a guy seems to know too much about handbags, he might be a generous fashion-forward kind of guy—or he is well versed in using them to impress women. His superficiality might also come in the form of bragging. Does he talk too much about money, whom he knows or what connections he has?

- Too affectionate too soon. You might think this is a desirable trait, but when affection comes too quickly, you should question the motive behind it. Mr. Insecure also tends to turn a date into a relationship too quickly.

- He is calling, texting and wanting to see you all the time. Insecure men don't just want to show you attention, they want to receive it in return, often questioning if you are not replying to a text message or call soon enough. While this may feel like attention, it is neediness, and there is a reason for it. They also want to take up as much of your time as possible, giving you little time to find or talk to someone else.

- He is controlling. He will try to tell you which of your friends he likes and doesn't like or make other decisions in your life for you. You might think this is his way of taking care of you, but in fact it is his way of controlling you. Controlling a woman can make a man feel more masculine.

- He rarely likes being alone, not because he enjoys the company of others, but because he needs people around to reinforce him and to boost his ego.

- Putting you down. Insecure men are out to pump themselves up and sometimes that means putting others (you) down. An insecure man has the ability to kill a woman's self-esteem. He does this because when she's down, she'll need exactly what he is offering: his love and approval. It can be a toxic cycle.

- Hidden anger. This is Mr. Insecure's most dangerous trait and sometimes it's a red flag for men who can be abusive. They might seem sweet and attentive on the outside, but if they feel like they are losing control, they can snap and explode in anger they can't suppress. Has he called you a mean name or given you a quick reaction (like grabbing your arm), and then followed it with an "I'm sorry, baby"? Has he stonewalled you for periods of time as an apparent punishment to teach you a lesson, ensuring you will toe the line again? When men are insecure and they don't get their own way, they can get frustrated. This frustration leads to emotional, psychological or even physical anger. This doesn't mean that every insecure man will turn abusive, but every man who is abusive is surely insecure.

Optimism: Your New Best Friend

However you choose to meet someone, there is one thing never to forget: optimism. If I wanted to buy into sayings like, "There are no good men left," I could, but it wouldn't get me anywhere. If you feel there is scarcity, you just might not be looking in the right places, giving off the right signals, flirting enough or giving enough of an invitation to be flirted with—you might not even be aware that someone is trying to get your attention.

Allowing negativity to get to you won't allow you to cultivate confidence and happiness, the two most important things to feel when you go out dating. When we decide to be optimistic, our thoughts and actions soon follow. You must believe that there are men out there in the universe and that the universe is conspiring to help you find them.

Chapter 6

Technosexually Savvy

Today, if you own a smartphone, you're carrying a 24/7 singles bar in your pocket.
—Aziz Ansari

As a modern SBD woman, it's important to stay on top of technological changes and platforms. Technology has changed the way we date, the way we talk and flirt with someone and even the way we have sex. It's opening up more doors, more legs, more opportunities and more accessibility to singles than ever before. We now readily express ourselves and our sexuality online, but we need to be aware of the indirect conversations and messages we are sending to others (especially potential dates) with what we say and post in the digital space. It's impossible to have set-in-stone rules when it comes to digital communication channels, as they are ever-changing, but technosexuality is about learning how to utilize technology in your own smart and sexy way for the highest good of your romantic and sexual life.

In the Beginning

God created man and woman—and then the smartphone. These little tech appendages have changed the way we date and erased nearly any semblance of mystery in the process. Before you even go out on a date with someone, you can get nearly their entire life's story from a few clicks.

What's That Supposed to Mean?

Be careful of reading too much into a text. Unless you know someone very well, it's nearly impossible to determine the tone they're using. The use of an "LOL" (laugh out loud) or an emoji can help, but if those symbols are left out, their message can feel like it means something altogether different. Don't go running to your friends to help you translate a text message from him, either; they, like you, probably aren't mind readers.

Because communication online and via text can have so many different interpretations, the rule of thumb I follow is: if you aren't sure, just go do something fun and wait for more interaction before you start to judge.

What's in a Reply?

The decision when to reply is a balancing act between being respectful enough to get back to someone when you can and actually being so busy that you're unable to for a bit. Don't use timing tactics as a way to keep him interested, though—

waiting to reply to keep him wondering is not nearly as good as actually living a life that keeps you genuinely and happily busy. Of course, if you are not interested, you may want to decrease how quickly and how often you reply to let him down slowly and gently.

When it comes to *what* to reply, consider the length of your texts, especially in the beginning. Just as it's advisable to keep it short in person with men, KISS is useful for online communication and texting, too. You don't want to be dating your phone, head constantly down, typing out your life story. You need to save something for dinner-date conversation or post-sex chitchat. Don't get me wrong: it's good to keep in touch and engage in playful banter; just don't get bogged down in lengthy conversations through your phone (which will turn you into a zombie and take away possible flirtatious eye glances with others) that you could have in person.

To Call or Not to Call

Text messages may have overtaken phone calls, but that doesn't mean people shouldn't still pick up the phone and connect with their voices. I've been told by many men that they quite enjoy it when a girl works up the courage to call, instead of trying to make plans via text, going back and forth a multitude of times just to organize dinner.

Text conversations can feel like they go on forever. If someone asks you a question or sends a text that requires a response, a reply should be sent back, but if it is just a statement that does not require a response, and the conversation has been going on for a bit, it can stop there. If there is more to be said, pick up the phone or save it for a face-to-face meeting.

Are You Being Rejected?

A clear rejection is always better than a fake promise.
—Unknown

Guys are not always as chatty on the phone or over text as girls, so consider whether his perceived brevity is really telling you that he is not that into you, or if he's just not a texting/phone type of guy. It's good to keep in touch and be playful while doing it, but there is a line where it's a little too much. Here is how you know when you have jumped over that line:

Go to your conversation with him in your phone and scroll up through the conversation history. If your text bubbles are always larger than his and there are significantly more of them, then it is time to chill and holster those thumbs. Women tend to want to talk and interact more than men (remember motor-mouth syndrome from Chapter 4?), but with phone banter, you want to try to be as equal as possible, so you know the other person is interested and engaging in the conversation with you. If he responds slowly or sends few messages back, often without any questions or statements that would require you to respond, then you know this is not the case and it might be time to let go. Remember, if he's into you, he will call and text you again.

A non-response speaks a thousand (or six) words: "I'm just not that into you." If you find yourself in this position, you may be dealing with a rude person, someone absorbed in his own world or just a bad fit. In any case, delete him from your phone and move on. That's hopefully not the type of guy you want to date.

If he gives "busy" as the reason he responds slowly or sometimes not at all, consider what message that sends you. He could be saying he is too busy *for you*. This is something only you can decide and the frequency with which he uses this reasoning will give you an indication of its true meaning.

If a guy is calling you, returning your calls, messaging you via text or email or sending carrier pigeons with notes, then he's into you. If he doesn't, then he's not. It's that simple. If you believe in yourself and your self-worth, then why are you wasting your time on someone who obviously doesn't value you in the same way?

There are exceptions to every rule and a reasonable person leaves room for "what-ifs" and benefit of the doubt. Maybe he left his phone in a cab or dropped it down the toilet and his contacts really did get wiped. Or maybe a magical dragon snatched the phone right out of his hands and flew away with it, but probably not. Use your common sense and look for patterns. Once or twice with no reply or the occasional slow response might not mean anything—he might just have a valid excuse—but if it's happening more than not, take the hint.

Being a smart SBD woman is about knowing how to both deliver and handle rejection. Instead of getting too upset, accept it, digest it, have a quick scream into your pillow or pint of ice cream if you must, then get back to focusing your energy on someone who is interested in you, which for the moment might even have to be yourself. If you have been working on your self-confidence and you have your emergency plan in place for when you feel down, then rejection should only sting slightly, because you have the right tools in place to kick it fast.

Too Much Tech

Consider the time you spend texting someone versus the time spent with them in person. Just like you may be saying too much online or in texts, you might also be painting a picture of someone in your head that isn't exactly true. We've all done this: created an entire future around someone because they are good at sending funny GIFs or deploy a couple of well-timed movie quotes.

In this way, dating apps and websites can work against us. You meet a guy online, he looks cute and sounds interesting and you start to project onto him your own perceptions of who you think he is or who you want him to be. You spend your time sending each other cute photos of what you are doing and start to build a relationship, protected by a screen.

This banter can make us laugh and feel so good that of course we must be in love and are going to live happily ever after. No. You aren't in love. You don't even actually know this person. You are wasting precious time IRL daydreaming about a fictional character you are creating through your handheld. Sorry to burst your bubble.

Think about why you are doing this. Often there is something going on in your life that you don't want to address and these kinds of distractions serve to pull your attention away so you don't have to deal with the thing that, more often than not, will get your life to a better place.

He Likes Me, He Likes Me Not

What's in a like?

Nothing.

Or maybe everything.

Either way, don't let "likes" make you too happy, too sad or too crazy. If a guy is really into you, he will call, email or text you, not just like your photos.

I once viewed someone's profile on LinkedIn who had the same name as my crush. He thought I was checking him out because he could see that I'd viewed him, so he hunted me down and insisted on taking me out for a date. It didn't work out, but I also never had the courage to tell him I hadn't been searching for him to begin with. Just as I so quickly viewed someone's profile, so can he press *like* on your status update. It doesn't necessarily mean he likes you; it just means that this update or photo appealed to him. Be careful not to take these quick online reactions as anything meaningful.

What You Don't Know You're Saying

Know that you are communicating with people when you are not aware of it. When you post and say things "publicly" online, you are telling a story about your life and what type of person you might be. You are also inadvertently helping people develop their estimation of you. When people—maybe some you don't even know very well—see photos, status updates or videos you post, they are constructing a perception of you according to the information they see. This perception might not be the real you or these photos might be further down your history and different from who you are today.

Is a guy you like not asking you out because he thinks you are vain, based on how many selfies you are posting? Is a guy booty calling you because your photos make you seem like a party girl? Is he not calling you back because your incessant complaining on FB makes you seem like a Debbie Downer? If someone was two years deep into your feed, what conclusions would they draw about you? Every so often, I will go through my social media and delete anything that no longer feels authentically me or that, on second thought, I wouldn't want my whole network judging me upon. This is also why I don't post as much personal content as I once did; people always used to think I lived this amazing life, traveling, boating and never working. The truth is that I was working more than ever! I just tended to post the fun stuff so it seemed that's all there was to me.

It's normal (and tempting) to post that good stuff, but beware of painting a false picture of yourself and your life online, and to the same point, remember not to jump to conclusions about other people's online content. It is best to think of your social media accounts as your personal calling cards—they advertise you and your life. It's fine if they are flattering, but make sure they are also authentic.

Can We Be Facebook Friends?

I always think it's best when you are first dating a guy or having a casual fling with him to refrain (for as long as possible) from interlocking your social media networks online. Especially if the nature of your relationship is uncertain or not monogamous, becoming "friends" online can cause trouble and send you to the loony bin. What happens if you see a photo of him with another girl, or if there is another girl commenting on his posts or liking all his photos? In a perfect world, being the confident SBD woman that you are, this shouldn't bother you, but we're all human. This type of information might not be good for your mental well-being. Maybe she's just a good friend from high school or his sister. Or maybe not. Maybe she is another woman he is having sex with or dating.

Becoming friends online is the technosexual version of taking your relationship to the next step, and you need to ask yourself, are you ready for the implications being friends online might bring? You don't want to find yourself at 2 a.m., stalking some random woman's brother's feed because you are trying to figure out if she is dating the same guy as you.

Dick Pics, a.k.a. Cock Shots

Sexting and dick pics (otherwise known as "cock shots") are everywhere. With this sexually explicit material, many times what you see is not what you get: often trading it is less a serious attempt to stimulate someone and more a game to see how much racy content you can convince another person to send. I've had friends show me texts they've received on their phones and it's mostly just good for a giggle.

I sit on the fence with this one. As crazy as it may sound, sexting and cock shots have become forms of modern-day courtship and can be a great way to have foreplay in the online world if done correctly. However, as with all advances in technology, there is a negative side: dick pics and sexting can lead to issues of distrust and even legal trouble. I'm not telling you to never send a sexy photo, but you have to know that whatever you send to someone, you need to be okay with the rest of the world seeing. I'm proud of my vulva, but that doesn't mean I'd want everyone I know sneaking a peek.

Have fun, but be smart. Be sure to serve up any naughty pics with a side of dignity. If it's an exchange with someone whom you are seeing or sleeping with, then some sexy visual aids might just add to the experience. If you have just met someone new, however, and they are asking for a racy pic, you might want to question if the request has come too soon. Has any trust been established? You don't want to be just another woman sending a naked pic to a guy who (let's be honest) could possibly share it with a group of his buddies over beers.

Sending Sexy Pics

In some circumstances, it's better and safer to send sexy pics than sext, especially if you don't know the person that well or have not been dating them for long. The difference being that sexting might involve the promise of sexual acts while a sexy pic (that does not show your face) might be something just to tantalize, showing off a little but not giving everything away. (When you have established trust, though, sexting can be a lot of fun.)

Consider requests for nude photos with common sense. A picture speaks a thousand words, so what does a nude selfie say? If you have just begun dating or have been chatting with someone without having been on a real date, this pic might tell him what type of relationship you are after. A flirty pic with your clothes on might say, "I'm fun, but you're gonna have to buy me dinner first," whereas a nude photo says, "It's just bedroom play that I'm after."

Pic Tips:

- First and most important, hide your face! Let me stress that by saying it once more: never let your face be visible in a sexy photo!
- Send something suggestive and sexy with *some* clothes on. This is a fun way to entice him.
- Pick one piece of your body to show him. If you show leg, don't show the goods up top, and vice versa.
- Be naked while not naked—it's possible to imply nudity when you are not actually nude. Maybe you have your hand over the right area or a sheet or object covering the bits that count.
- Before you send it, ask him not to show anyone else. Your request will not guarantee that this will be the case, but I think it's important to at least let him know that you are seriously attempting to put a boundary in place.
- Even once you've taken the photo, don't feel pressured to press send. Do it because you want to, not because you feel you have to. You can take a sexy pic just for yourself, too.

Don't ever feel bullied into sending something you don't feel comfortable with. Once again, this may come down to you wanting to feel accepted and liked—his request might get stronger over time or he may even taunt you with words like "boring" or "prudish." This is a boundary you do not want to give in on. Ever. No matter how much you like him, this is not an area to take risks or do things that make you feel uncomfortable in any way. To be crystal clear, you do not have to send anything of a sexual nature in order to have a guy like you. You should do it only if you genuinely want to, feel comfortable and it excites you.

A less serious negative to this trend is that if you receive a dick pic, you've ruined the surprise of seeing a guy's member. It's like knowing what your Christmas present is before you open it or knowing the end of the book before you've finished it. This can take away the feeling of excitement associated with a first sexual encounter. If this is a concern for you, maybe you want to let him know that you don't want to receive a dick pic. Alternatively, maybe you want to see the merchandise before you commit. Either way, just be tuned in to your own personal preferences, communicate them and stay true to you.

Virtual Sex

Whether it's mutual masturbation over Skype or FaceTime or sending a continual series of sexual images and words, virtual sex carries implications similar to sexting and should be done with just as much respect. With virtual sex, I feel that we are able to take things further and experience bonding emotions, intimacy and connections similar to those that would occur in real-life sexual experiences. Unlike sexting with our phones, with something like Skype or FaceTime, the only thing between people is literally the screen. You can hear and see (but not touch) a person as you would in real life, so you can get attached to someone you are having regular virtual sex with.

The Ugly Side to Sexting

A guy I was dating allowed me into a folder on his phone that contained 20-odd women's names with more folders full of naked and sexual shots. There were ex-girlfriends, girls he had dated casually, random girls and everything in between. These were not just shots of vulvas and boobs. These were graphic images of sexual acts and legs wide open with nothing left to the imagination.

I came across one name, Kelly, and as I clicked on the folder, it too was full of naked, raunchy photos. The way he spoke about her—as though she were just another pair of tits—and the way he proudly showed me these photos saddened me and made me think I would hate to see my name on a folder in someone's phone, boasted about like a sexual souvenir instead of being praised as the sensual woman I am. Our naked bodies are beautiful and precious, and anyone who treats them in any other manner should not have the privilege of seeing or touching any piece of them.

In this instance, sexuality seemed it had gone down the drain and meant very little. Was this the effect of our techno-sexual culture making us so replaceable? If one girl won't send a naked photo of herself or her genitals, then it is easy enough to find someone who will.

One might think that in order to send a shot like this you need to have pretty healthy self-esteem. In many cases, that is true, but I also think the opposite is true and the willingness with which these are sent might indicate a woman's lack of self-esteem. Sexually explicit photos and messages are another avenue where women can get validation and an ego boost from men, but sending them for that reason shows us a woman hasn't created a strong-enough sense of self on her own.

Sexting is a part of our culture, so it's important that we fully understand what happens to these images, why someone wants them, what they could do with them and what the consequences might be if they are made public. If we are aware of all these elements, we can accept sexting for what it is and allow it into our lives in the appropriate ways.

Sexting and virtual sex can be a lot of fun with the right person (which is a respectful person). When in a relationship or even while dating or casually hooking up, I love to use technology to have a bit of flirty or sexy banter. It excites me, excites him and makes me look forward to what's to come or reminds me what we have been up to. Try to keep in mind that these exchanges should be something sexy to lead him on and leave him wanting more; there is no need to show him where your birth canal is.

It's Complicated

I make it a blanket rule never to change my relationship status on Facebook or even to list it as Single. (If only we had the option of Single but Dating!) If you want to know whom I'm dating or what's going on in my life, call me and ask. If you don't have my number, then maybe we're not friends at all and you don't deserve to know. If I don't put things all over social media—which can lead to worry over what to post or not to post, who will comment, etc.—then I'm more easily able to live in the moment in a relationship. In a world where everyone seems to share everything online, it's nice to keep these things private so they can evolve more naturally IRL. I have added so many random people over the years to my FB account that I can't even remember who they all are (some probably from nights out drinking). Why would I want everyone, especially those for whom "friend" is a term used loosely, knowing my intimate personal life? It might not be like this forever, but I do think that at the start of a relationship, keeping those you're romantically linked to offline is a good idea. If I take a photo with someone I'm seeing, I'll send it to a select few people who might care (and always my mum). This not only keeps me more present with the person I'm with but also helps me to stay connected to my inner circle of friends. My photos are for memories and to share with those I love, not for everyone I've ever met to make up their own conclusions about my life and likely think it's something that it's not.

When dating, keep the status of your phone and your social media accounts in mind. It can be a good idea to turn your phone on silent, take off notifications from dating apps, stop messages coming through on a locked screen and keep any relationship statuses online questionable. It's a privilege to be living in an SBD world, but not everyone will understand it and you might eventually change your mind or move on to a committed relationship. The term SBD is an attempt at a label that is freeing, so don't give any information online that will confine you or define you. Technology is a great tool in the dating game, but it can also be the death of mystery or used as a crutch. It's being technosexually savvy to ditch unnecessary alerts, functions and features on social media so you can be as comfortable face to face as you are through a screen.

Chapter 7

Mind Your Manners

*What is a date, really, but a job interview that lasts
all night? The only difference is there aren't many
job interviews where you'll wind up naked.*
—Jerry Seinfeld

The dating landscape may have changed, but this doesn't mean
we need to let bad behaviors run rampant. Chivalry is not, and
should never be, dead. When people engage in casual hookups,
random sex and online dates, respect and manners can seem
to go out the window. The fact is, if you are going to be intimate with someone, respect should be shown regardless of
the dating situation. We should be as considerate to those we
hook up with casually as we would be with anyone else. You
never know: you might want to hook up with them again in the
future, or one day their opinion of you could be a deal-breaker
for another potential relationship, or even in your professional
life; it is a small world, after all.

I'm afraid I can't stop men from disrespecting you, but you
can, and I can tell you how to set the tone for a respectful
encounter, casual fling or date.

Men tend to get our desire for respect mixed up with commitment. Wanting to be respected does not necessarily mean

that we want to be in a relationship. If this is the case for you, remember our discussion of communication in Chapter 4. There can be a gray area in the SBD world, so be clear about your intentions and wishes for a given relationship.

Getting respect from others starts with showing yourself respect. Respecting yourself means you don't date, bed or let someone take up your time who doesn't hold the same view of you.

Setting the Scene, SBD Style

There is nothing wrong with having purely sexual intentions. If a first date is hanging at his place, grabbing a drink or watching a movie on the couch, a casual sexual relationship or hookup is in the cards. I'm personally a fan of the "Netflix and chill" code—it sounds nicer than "Hey, wanna fuck?" You always have a right to say no or push his hands off you, so if your "movie night" is turning into "moving too fast for your liking night," you can always just actually watch the movie.

If there is no mention of a movie and you're just having a late-night visit, this most likely means casual sex only. Dinner normally indicates an official date, however what happens after dinner might be more telling.

If you are out to drinks with a guy you like and the invitation to come home with him appears, don't freak out as though casual sex is all he is offering. He is just a guy and most guys *will* try to take you home or make some sexual advance. It's in their DNA. If you want something more with him, all you need to say is, "Not tonight, but I would love to catch up again." You can also turn the corner to official-dates-ville when the suggestion of a movie night is made. All you need to reply is, "How about we grab a bite to eat instead?" If you find yourself on an official date and were really only looking for something casual, invite him back to yours, touch his leg or be cheeky enough to let those intentions be known. It's that simple.

One dating trap can be when a first date takes the form of a bedroom visit, and only after do you realize that you actually may want something more. If this happens to you, don't worry—hooking up and casual sex are also forms of dating these days. You can always suggest that the next meeting be over dinner. Be aware, however, that if you've already been sexual, there is the expectation of a repeat performance. If you want to go back to taking things slow, you certainly have that right; you just need to be honest with him about it (while reassuring him you are still keen).

The First Date

Sometimes it can be useful for a first date to include an activity for you both to focus on, especially if you suffer from first-date nerves. Try to choose something where you can still get a chance to talk to each other (but talking to each other is not all you have to do): a wine tasting, street fair, theme park, a sporting activity like stand-up paddle-boarding or hiking, watching a sporting game, a day at the beach or a visit to an art gallery are all good options. The key is choosing something that you will both enjoy and can bond over, which requires a little bit of effort and gives the opportunity to see how you both interact in other situations. Going to the movies is not the best first or even second date, as you are sitting in a dark room unable to talk to or even see each other.

The timing of your dates and the plans to have them might tell you a bit more about the person you are seeing. If a guy is into you, he will make plans with you well in advance. Being an SBD woman doesn't mean hanging around for the phone to ring. It means living your life and accepting offers when they come by. Don't wait around for a better offer; say yes—even if it's to a catch-up with the girls!

There is a big difference between "I want to see you" and "My plans have fallen through, so you will do." A last-minute request should be analyzed with caution. If you are a confident woman, why would you be free at a moment's notice on a Friday or Saturday night, when these are the prime dating and socializing nights? More than likely, you'd have plans. Being spontaneous and going with the flow can be fun, but make sure his request is not actually insulting. If you've been dating someone a bit longer, a last-minute catch-up might be acceptable, but don't give anyone the impression you were waiting by the phone.

If this request is for a casual hookup, then you really can't complain; after all, it's casual. But you need to decide if he's reached out because he was thinking of you and his attraction to you was on his mind, or if he was just in the mood for sex and you were next on his list. Even in the case of a casual relationship, the latter may feel insulting. Only you can decide when the timing doesn't feel right.

Free Your Mind

Because we live in such a superficial, fast-paced dating world, our judgments on a first date can be harsh and swift. It can be brutal, so it's important we open our minds and get to know someone, regardless of the food in their teeth or their bad choice of outfit.

Just as I can encourage you not to be so judgmental on a first date, I should warn you that unfortunately your date might still be judgmental of you. You should assume that he's watching your every move—or worse, watching his phone for a better offer. The catch-22 here is that stress can be your worst enemy, keeping you from being the best version of you, so despite all this scary stuff, you do in fact need to relax.

Everyone will have their own list of dating deal-breakers and you probably won't know what they are. You might like to think that he sees you as a nice person and accepts you just the way you are, but realistically that is more often the case on a second, third or fourth date, once he has actually gotten to know you. On a first date, unfortunately the judgment is on.

If you are so nervous that you feel you are not being your best self, why not own it? At least that way you'll both be able to excuse some of the things that happen as a reflection of your nerves and not on the amazing person you really are. Be understanding that he could also be nervous, especially because there is more of an expectation for him not to be, as he is the man in the scenario. Strong, powerful SBD women can be a little intimidating to men and it might take him a while to find his dating confidence, so go easy. If you pick up on his nerves, try to be kind and caring, not harsh and impatient. Nerves should not be a dating deal-breaker; they should just be identified so you know the difference between the effect they're having and your date's usual personality.

Dress for Sexcess

Make sure you do your research before choosing an outfit for a date. The venue is the biggest indicator of what to wear. You don't want to go somewhere too overdressed or turn up too casual. Simply do a quick Google search to find out what the place is like.

Consider what message your clothes will send. There is a balance between sexy and smart. My rule of thumb—flaunt only one asset! Choose to show your legs, shoulders or your cleavage—but don't show them all at once!

Always make sure you wear something that not only looks good but that makes you feel good, too. Also, be careful of how much makeup you wear. Of course you want to look nice, but too much cakey-makey can be a big turnoff to a guy. An overload of makeup can send a guy the message that we are insecure about what we look like underneath.

Shoes can present a dilemma. Most women do not like to tower over men and, in return, most men don't like it when a woman towers over them. If this is a blind date, an online/app date or a setup, try to guess how tall he is by looking at his profile photos (pro tip: pics where he is standing near a doorway offer a good point of comparison). I once stood up after a drink only to realize I was taller than the guy. I also wore flats on another blind date and had the guy tower over me at an uncomfortable distance when heels would have made me feel better. Do a little research.

This last element could determine if the night ends in a kiss (or a little more): lipstick. As much as red lips might look sexy, they can be a total kissing turnoff. If a guy wants to kiss you, he will, but if he is shy, nervous or conscious of how red lipstick will look on him, he might wait to make his move. This may sound silly, but I truly believe that if you want a goodnight kiss, stick to a little colored lip gloss and save the red lips for another time.

If you are going for a casual hookup, don't stress too much about clothing, as I'm sure it won't be on too long. For this, focus more on what underwear makes you feel good and brings out your sexual goddess side.

Conversational No-No's

On dates, try to avoid talking about: past lovers, boyfriends or spouses; money; religion; politics; or bodily functions. There is always an exception to the rule; if the conversation naturally turns to a point where you are both talking about religion (or poop), then it might show a sign of comfort to be able to partake (especially if you are talking about poop). But as a general rule, try to keep away from these topics.

Be careful not to talk too much about your deal-breakers. First dates are for getting to know each other enough to decide whether you want to see each other for a second date, not the time to rattle off your dating wish list.

Talking about sex is an easy way to get someone's attention, but, on a first date, if you want to get to know the person beyond bed, talking too much about sex can work against you. (Because sex is the subject of my job, this one slips me up every time!) If you talk about sex a lot, he might think that's all you are after. However, if you are only after sex, then you can use this to your advantage.

Alcohol

Alcohol can be your best friend and your worst enemy. Two glasses of wine can be great to lower inhibitions just enough so you are able to let your good side shine, but too much and you might be a blubbering mess or end up going home with him when you didn't want to. It's important to know your limits.

The limit on alcohol for a casual hookup is not drinking so much that you can't actually proceed sexually or can be pushed into doing things you wouldn't otherwise be comfortable with. I actually find that a couple of well-timed drinks can help you relax and can even help women achieve an orgasm. But too many and not only might your sexual boundaries be crossed but your safer-sex plans could go awry.

Just because you are with someone for a casual hookup does not mean you are certainly going to engage in penis–vagina sex. If this is a boundary you don't want to cross, you have every right not to cross it, even if you have made a commitment to have a casual hookup. With too much alcohol in your system (which can make your vulva speak louder than your head), this might be an easy decision to renege on. With lowered inhibitions and Ms. Vulva driving the bus, consequences usually aren't properly considered.

The Kiss Dilemma

A kiss is what really seals the deal. Some people don't believe in kissing on the first date, but I certainly do. How else do you know if it's just a friendly catch-up or if they really want to see you again? It's all in the kiss.

That last goodbye at the end of the night has the potential to be oh-so-awkward. If you are into him, give him ample chance to get in there with a snog. For example, a lean in or the opportunity to walk you home or to your car is helpful. If you are not keen, go in firmly with a kiss on the cheek or a hug. A hug is usually the safer choice here (the kind where you pat him on the back like a mom would), as there is always an awkward meeting of faces when you give him your cheek and he aims for your lips. Once again, your actions should express your future intentions, so if you don't want to see him again, make sure to add after that hug or kiss on the cheek "Thanks for a lovely night," but don't include "We should do it again."

Safety First

Safety is paramount in the SBD dating world. In the modern and digital dating landscape, we are meeting more and more people, agreeing to go out with them for dinner, catching up with them over coffees and drinks and even bedding them without knowing who they really are.

This is not to say that every stranger you meet is going to be harmful, but there really isn't a way to tell one way or another without time to know each other. You need to be careful of the amount of alcohol you consume, as it will affect how you see the situation. Always go somewhere public and let a friend or family member know where you are and whom you are with. If you don't feel right *for any reason,* leave! If you need to, excuse yourself to the bathroom and call a friend to come and get you. There is a big difference between feeling awkward and feeling unsafe.

I once wanted a casual hookup to leave my apartment but didn't quite have the guts back then to tell him directly to leave. It was not a safety issue but more of an irritation issue. I texted my bestie, who was at a bar, to call me back. She rang in a "dramatic state" and said she needed me at the bar right away, so I hurriedly got dressed and asked my casual hookup to drop me in the city so I could go and help her. I walked into the bar, downed the glass of champagne that my friend had waiting for me and went straight back to bed (on my own). That's what friends are for.

With a casual hookup whom you've met on an app or online, safety might be a bigger risk. You'll meet them in public, but you also need to use your gut to determine whether going home with them is a good idea. (Casual hookups are safer under a "friends with benefits" circumstance. More on that later.)

Check, Please!

There is often awkwardness when it comes to who will pay the bill. It's a dance. You offer to pay half but sometimes you don't really mean it and are just trying to be polite. If he were to take you up on your offer, you might be offended, but then how can you be when you offered in the first place? Why don't we just admit that women enjoy men paying for them on dates, especially the first one? It's got nothing to do with their financial earnings; it's much more about old-fashioned dating etiquette. This doesn't mean that the man should pay for every date, and you should work out how to send the message that his financial support is not all you are after. Maybe you can offer to pay for the drinks at the next bar or for the taxi, take him out for dessert, bring the bottle of wine and takeaway next time or grab the movie tickets. It's not a matter of splitting the cost of each meal, but old-fashioned manners mixed with modern-day female empowerment and a girl's ability to pay her own way.

Doing the No Pants Dance Before Romance

There is one question we can never answer: when is the right time to have sex? These days, when sex is often delivered to a man on a silver platter, there is much more of an expectation for sex on a date. When an SBD woman is out dating, having fun and not putting the serious-relationship hat on, a guy might assume that sex should be part of the equation straight away.

I feel the need to make it clear that women today are free to have one-night stands and we need to celebrate that. It is exciting that we are liberated enough to engage in something that has until now been considered taboo. If you do want to engage in this type of sexual activity, you need to understand where the desire comes from, what's involved and what possible consequences there are, so you can make an informed decision (and not just a horny one). Sex can be risky, both emotionally and physically, so it's not asking too much to want to know a bit about the person you are taking that risk with.

I know it's natural for men to desire sex straight away when dating, but an internal battle rages for a woman. On one side are biology and desire; on the other is consequence. If there were no consequences to having sex on a first date, more women would be doing it and enjoying it. Perhaps men are to blame for this waiting game. Who out there has had sex on the first, second or third date, then never heard from the guy again? Or only heard from him in the context of a booty call? Although it's never said aloud, the refrain seems to be: "I'll sleep with you if you give it up straight away, but it means you're a slut and I won't date you seriously. If you make me wait, you are a good girl and I'll pursue a relationship with you." Again, there are exceptions to this rule—I know a number of long-term relationships that began with sex straight away—but it's still a belief held by some. It isn't fair, but sometimes women are forced into those categories: Miss Relationship or Miss Sexual. We can and have the right to be both.

This is one of the problems with being an SBD woman. As an SBD woman, there is a place for you and men for you to date, but unfortunately there are those who believe these fun and liberating situations are dirty or immoral. That may not change, but you can control how you respond to it. Don't let anyone make you feel guilty about the choices you have happily and confidently made in your dating and sex lives. If you do make mistakes, learn from them. But take any shame associated with them and flush that right down the toilet.

Sex with an Agenda

As we mentioned earlier in Sex as a Weapon, some women think sex will fast-track the dating process into a relationship or that by making him wait for sex, he will work harder and stick around longer. Both of these scenarios can go horribly wrong. Sex with an agenda other than pleasure, fun and connection can be like using the wrong tool to build something: it probably won't work very well and will probably have negative consequences.

In many situations, I don't think women withhold sex for lack of want, but rather from fear of the consequences if they do give in to their sexuality. Fear is a tactic used to control women, especially when it comes to sex, and we need to acknowledge this fear exists and learn to recognize when it rears its ugly head. You might be waiting because you want to get to know him better, to feel more connected, to feel comfortable being naked with him, to know his sexual history or simply to have something to look forward to in a new relationship or dating scenario. You might also be waiting because you are fearful of what he might think if you give it up too soon—regardless of the fact that he wants it, too.

I can offer up lots of reasons why you should do what you want sexually, but deep down we all know that our natural urges and sexual choices can be used against us. It's not right, but it's true. For some men, the exact thing they're asking for is the one thing that can halt the possibility of a future relationship or more dates. All because you have given them what they wanted!

We are going for agenda-free sex in the ideal SBD world, so do it when your intuition tells you it's right. Just be aware that sex early on can also have negative consequences, and know why they exist and how to navigate them. In the same way that age is just a number, so, too, is the number of dates you have before sex. It's what's going on emotionally that counts, no matter how long you've known each other.

Playing the Field

It's really hard to maintain a one-on-one relationship if the other person is not going to allow me to be with other people.
—Axl Rose

When you start dating someone, don't assume that you are off the market from the first date or from the first time you sleep together. Until you have a conversation about dating exclusively and not seeing other people, assume that one person could be hanging the "off the market" sign while the other is still online hunting for new dates.

There are situations when dating multiple men can be a lifesaver for a woman. When you date just one guy you like, it's not hard to get tunnel vision or even mildly obsessed with him. If you were dating three men, let's say, you'd be so busy talking to one that you wouldn't even notice that the other hadn't called you all day or had been slow to reply to a text message. The key is to be focused enough to get to know him and distracted enough not to think about him every moment. Dating multiple people is not always the ideal way to really get to know someone on an intimate level, but it is a great way to stay sane before you do.

Dating multiple men is also a great way to slow down the dating process and keep things casual, which, as an SBD woman, may be your goal. If the dating process is slower, you have more time to sexperiment and sexplore.

Dating multiple people also keeps us somewhat unavailable, which isn't a bad thing. As we've discussed, being an SBD woman is not about just appearing unavailable; it is about actually being unavailable because you have a full and fulfilling life. This has the added benefit of sending the message that if he wants you, he'll have to pick up his game. This is not being dishonest—it's what dating in the digital age is all about.

But what happens if he bumps into you while you are on another date? What if it turns out that you have friends in common with someone you're dating? The "I like you and want to continue dating you, but, just to let you know, I can't be monogamous with you yet" conversation may be awkward, but when you are dating multiple men, make sure you are forthright.

Imagine you've met a great guy but he doesn't tick all your boxes. If you don't want to get married and have children next week, why give up spending time with another great Mr. Right Now or two? This is what's great about the SBD time in your life—you are on the market and available for new experiences. If you are not dating just one guy in the hope of getting married, you are able to spend time with many people who can add value to your life.

Taking Yourself Off the Market Too Soon

Unless you are in an official and exclusive relationship, then you are always on the market in some way. There are a number of reasons a woman runs the risk of prematurely appearing to be off the market when she is not: because life is busy, perhaps it is winter and you aren't up for going out as much or maybe you're just feeling a little lazier in the dating game. If you want to leave your options open, however, make sure you continue to live your life.

If you're not up for balancing multiple men but want to practice an SBD life, make sure you date one man as if you have others on the side—with a bit of distance, a bit of distraction and without the need to be with him every second of the day. When you're dating one person, aside from it being easy to start obsessing, it's also easy to get too comfortable and fall into the trap of being in a relationship that isn't quite right— because he's nice and it's easier than having to end it and really be on your own.

It's Been Real

Whether you've been dating someone for a few days, a few weeks, or even just casually hooking up with them, breakups can be downright confusing. It might not be a breakup in the traditional sense (because you weren't traditionally dating), but when a connection of some sort has been formed and one or both people involved want to break that connection, ending it can still feel like a breakup.

You might be dating someone with whom you don't want to spend the rest of your life but who, right now, provides company you enjoy. If you are adopting this casual let's-just-see-where-it-goes attitude but know deep inside that he is not the right one for you, be careful if it becomes apparent that he thinks you might just be the right one for him. It's terrible form to lead people on. Being a dick in your SBD life will never make you feel good in the long run, so if you sense your levels of interest are disparate, it's your time to call it quits or at least be honest about how you feel and let him make an informed decision.

Unfortunately, toxic and/or dramatic breakup scenarios do happen—they are par for the course. Whether you are dating casually or hooking up, you might put up with negative behavior because you know the guy you're seeing is not the marrying kind, not your full-time boyfriend and only right for a bit of fun. This can be okay for a while, depending on how bad his behavior is. Eventually, though, the negatives will outweigh the positives and that's when you have to be realistic. When your tears (or angry faces) outweigh your smiles, it's time to get out, no matter how hot, good in bed or funny he might be.

How you end this kind of relationship should depend on the amount of time you have been seeing him and how intimate things have become. If you were casually dating, you don't want to make it sound like you thought there was something there that wasn't by giving him some official breakup speech. If you were dating, try something like, "Hi, I just want to let you know I've really enjoyed your company over the past few weeks but I don't think we are right for each other/don't see this going anywhere/think we are probably better off as friends/don't feel the spark/am moving to Poland." If you break up with someone who has been nice to you, don't forget to tell him that. If it's a hookup you are ending, you can opt for rejection or you can just slow things down to the point it fizzles out. No matter the situation, if you need out, be honest about it: "I don't think I can do this anymore, but I had a lot of fun" or "I think we should probably just be platonic friends for now" have worked for me. Remaining platonic friends with a hookup buddy can be a great way to call upon them again when you do feel in the mood or get over whatever it was they were doing.

Then, there is *ghosting*. Ghosting is when someone you've been seeing, speaking to or hooking up with just up and disappears—and it never feels nice. When a person is ghosted, they are often left very confused and sometimes even continue to send requests to catch up, as they have not received a direct message of rejection. Should you ever ghost someone else? Sometimes it may feel easier to ghost than to make that awkward call or text, especially if there has only been one or two dates. I'm not going to say that there is never a situation when ghosting is appropriate, but if you do decide to do it, really consider how it will make the other person feel.

Recycle Dating

Because many apps use your location to match you, many swipes occur in a certain radius from your home or work, and that all but guarantees you will end up dating the same guy as a friend, an acquaintance or a friend of a friend. This means that odds are, if you are dating lots of people in one particular part of the world, you are going to come across the ex of someone you know, or you will be the ex of one of your date's friends. Someone is bound to come in contact with your ex, too— but one girl's trash is another's treasure, and this is all part of "recycle dating."

Recycle dating can hold interesting implications for female friendships. When you are dating and hooking up with multiple men in the same city as your friends, there is a good chance that you and at least one of your friends will have slept with or dated some of the same men. If this happens, you are what I like to call "dick sisters." (Men who have this in common call themselves "Eskimo brothers.") This can't be helped, so don't freak out if it happens to you and certainly don't allow it to affect your friendships. Just because you went out on one or two dates with a guy or hooked up with him once does not mean he is off the market to your friends. If it didn't work out between the two of you, then why stop it from working out for someone else? If you are aware that a friend has dated a guy who is asking you out, you may want to touch base with her first. However, it's often the case that you won't be aware how your paths and vaginas have crossed until after the fact.

If you do realize you are dating a guy your friend has been out with, consider how much information you really want to know about them. You might want her to tell you if he is certified psycho, but her tiffs with him might not be relevant and may only put a bad taste in your mouth. You are different people and it's wise to make up your own mind on any guy whom you have both dated. Consider this also if a friend is dating someone you have been with. Is your information warning her of someone harmful or stopping her from getting to know someone through her own experiences?

Recycle dating is a great reason to consider carefully how you end any dating scenario, as you never know when an ex's opinion might be valued by a new date, or when your friend might start dating a guy you once did. Thanks to Facebook, when you start dating someone new, you are able to see the friends that you both have in common. You are also able to see which (one or more!) of his friends you have dated and slept with (something you should consider when pondering whether or not to add Mr. Right Now on Facebook). If you have been in a relationship with one of his friends, then you should probably mention it. If you had a one-night stand, a casual fling or just briefly dated someone on your "mutual friends" list, you'll need to consider: what might it look like if one of his buddies gets to him with this information first? You should probably be up front about it when the timing feels right. If you are having casual sex and one-night stands with men, then you might just come across a guy who is friends with someone, or more than one person, you have been with. Whether he will view this as a deterrent if he finds out is up to him.

Negative Nancy

Women in groups can sometimes be quite negative, moaning and groaning about the bad men in their life and the woes of being single; this can really rub off on your positive mood! Also, when we hear that one of our female folk is upset because she has been hurt by a man, we tend to go straight to party lines: "You are so much better than that/him," or "Get rid of him" or "He doesn't know what he has." This is well-meaning advice given by friends who love and care for you and don't want to encourage you to stay with someone who makes you upset. However, keep in mind that we often tell our friends when things don't work out, not when things do, which can give them a very negative impression of our dates from which they formulate their advice. Also, if they tell you to "walk away," they might not respond well if you do go back for more. Don't be or indulge in the Negative Nancy side when you talk about relationships. Learn which women you can confide in with everything and which ones you might need to censor some facts around. This might be the difference between a good friend and a great friend.

Chapter 8

(Man)Handling SBD Situations

Just because someone is single doesn't mean they're lonely.
Some people are in relationships and they've
forgotten what happiness is.
—Drake

You might want to consider that hookups, booty calls and friends with benefits are new avenues for dating and increasingly considered norms. These are types of relationships that allow SBD women to have multiple men in our lives and enjoy our sexploration.

Casual Sex and Hooking Up

The exact definition of a casual hookup relationship can be broad and is very much up to the individuals involved. There can be a lot of gray area; for example, is it casual sex or just casual non-penetrative sexual acts? One thing is clear, however: a casual hookup is not a relationship and might not even mean you are dating. A casual hookup could be a great way to test the waters with someone to see if there is chemistry before you begin dating, or it may serve as a way to have fun indefinitely without strings attached.

One-Night Stands

I like to refer to one-night stands as "one-night specials"—because why can't spending just one night with someone be special? In the past, a one-night special was pretty much the most taboo thing a woman could do. Now, although there are social stigmas attached, of course, one-night specials in the SBD world are actually pretty common.

Even so, one-night specials are still frowned upon by some. It could be the risk involved or because it damages the good-girl persona some believe a woman should embody; a good girl isn't supposed to want sex so much that she's willing to have it on a one-night stand, is she? This is an old-fashioned thought as well as a double standard. Sex can be a beautiful, amazing experience between a couple or even friends, but it can be just as much fun with someone you've recently met or hardly know. Women are sexual and have sex drives just like men—so sometimes a girl just needs to get laid.

I enjoy the connection and intimacy that come with having a partner, but in order to come to this realization, I had to experience what having one night of pleasure and drama was all about. If you are having a one-night special and you think there might be something more, it's always better to under-assume than over-assume. One-night specials should not be a way to get a guy to like you, although that's not to say feelings can't grow naturally from them. Be realistic and present in the pleasurable moment of a one-night special without trying to turn it into a future. If that happens anyway, it happens.

The difficult thing (that you might only discover afterward) is finding out if you are the type of person who can engage in a one-night special. A one-night special is a little like having anal sex: you will never know if you like it until you try it. For some, the one-night special is an occasional (or even common) scenario that turns out to be something they enjoy, but if you feel empty, lonely or upset when he walks out of that room, then maybe it's time to consider whether this sexual experience is for you. Either way, don't feel bad about testing it out. Everyone is different and so are their sexual needs and preferences. Sometimes you have to let yourself be an experiential learner and move right along to the next sexploration that might resonate more with you.

The biggest risk with this sexual act of a one-night special (which doesn't have to include penetration, by the way) is that technically you are inviting a stranger into your home and between your legs. You might already know him, but the chances are if you do, you don't know him well. There is usually little time to discuss sexual histories or contraception. There is no safeguard against this; it's a risk you have to understand you will be taking. You can minimize that risk by not engaging in a one-night special with someone who is too drunk (including you) or under the influence of drugs, always using condoms (which of course you know are not 100 percent effective), always telling a friend where you are going and whom you are going with and, most important, if you don't feel right for any reason, leaving, asking him to leave or calling for help.

Booty Calls

The real art of a booty call lies in navigating the fine line between using someone for sexual fun and just plain using them. The complex thing is that, technically, on a booty call, both people involved *are* using each other for something, but using respect even in this circumstance is a must.

If you get a call from a guy very late at night, you have to consider that he might have made other calls before he called you, which can leave you wondering what number you were on his list. For this reason, I think it's better for a woman to be the booty caller than the booty callee—that way, you have your own list and are calling the shots.

A good trick is putting your booty call feelers out ahead of time. Before you go out or when you think you will soon be in the mood, shoot off a text along the lines of "Hey, what are you up to later tonight?"—it's like bumping yourself to the top of his list and penciling in a booty call ahead of time. Because it's not an official plan, there is always room for a better offer if one arises. This tactic also leaves room for you to decline when the time comes, with something like, "I'm sorry, I am too tired/have to feed my friend's cats/am a drunk mess and not in the good way" and so on. This might sound harsh, but we are talking about the art of the booty call, not an official date. Just as you might be pulling this move with him, so might he be doing it with you. Self-esteem is important in the world of booty calls, and if you make sure you have it, this won't faze you.

If a booty call evolves into something more regular (like with all repeated casual situations), there is a risk of feelings developing, and with that risk comes the responsibility to discuss it.

It's only natural when a woman sleeps with a guy, even just once, that her hormones respond. As I mentioned before, false intimacy can blind us and lead us to think we are experiencing real love instead of just attraction. Have sex with the same guy more than once and the chances of this happening begin to skyrocket. Be aware of this and remind yourself that the relationship began casually for a reason. Anything more is by no means off limits if you want to mutually explore it, but don't go living in fantasy land thinking that it's something it's not when you haven't established that.

There was once a guy I had a fling with who, after a few months of not seeing each other, invited me out to dinner. The fantasy part of my brain thought he might be ready to give a relationship an actual go with me. It became clear that the reality was different when, during dinner, he told me with a grin, "I think we should be friends with benefits." We hooked up while both on holiday and I probably was not able to truly see who he was. Until that point at least. Sometimes reality slaps you in the face after fantasy sends you floating to the clouds.

I used to hook up with a guy whom I struggled to develop a relationship with for various reasons. I was attracted to him and enjoyed spending time with him when it was just the two of us—I would actually go through cycles where, after spending lots of bedroom time alone with him, I'd convince myself it was true love. Each time this happened, I would only get hurt and feel rejected when our time couldn't translate to the outside world. After a few weeks, I'd eventually go back, having convinced myself I was only returning for the sex, only to have history repeat itself—and leave me feeling hurt and disappointed—once again.

Our bodies can play cruel tricks on us when we have sex because, in some ways, our biology still thinks sex is for procreation. Therefore, the side effect of bonding with someone our body thinks we are to have a baby with can come involuntarily after the sexual act. Step away from the man and look at the situation—are your current feelings just a side effect of bonding induced by sex or are they something different?

Friends with Benefits (FWB)

In a FWB scenario, there will probably be more of a connection because you know the person better and will be seeing them more often, both inside the bedroom and outside in normal, friendly situations. FWB doesn't have to be with someone you socialize with outside of the bedroom and could just mean you see them casually for hookups on a repeat basis.

There are many reasons that a FWB scenario might begin. Maybe there is a sexual attraction with this person but it wouldn't work out as anything more. Maybe it is simply a convenient arrangement between friends who already see each other socially and aren't looking for relationships. Maybe the FWB scenario feels like a safer sexual option, as, you would hope due to your established friendship, there is a deeper level of trust and communication that enables you to discuss important sexual issues and concerns.

The biggest risk with a FWB situation, especially if the friendship has begun as a close one, is that turning it sexual could ruin the original friendship. Will this friendship stand the tests of sexual tension, potential drama or unreciprocated feelings developing? Before you cross the line from friends to FWB, consider if you'd be upset losing the friendship or if you're okay fucking that friendship away.

In order for these special friendships to last, unfortunately, you just might have to do that one thing you thought being in this type of relationship saved you from: communicate. These situations can be very fun and fulfilling, but they also come with gray area and emotional risks.

Consider how you will feel if your FWB is dating other people and you realize you want him just for yourself. There can be awkwardness if one person develops feelings and the other doesn't. If you do develop feelings, you might find yourself getting jealous but feeling unable to voice those feelings due to the "casual" nature of a FWB relationship. Lots of feelings and no place to express them? That's enough to make you crazy.

Ensure you discuss the boundaries and expectations of your individual FWB situation. Even though you'd think the "benefits" include not having to talk about emotions, if things start to feel complicated but the sex is still good, you'll want to set some parameters: e.g., you only see each other a certain number of times, you take a break if things become too intimate or if you're feeling too connected or you don't ask questions about each other's dating life.

FWB can be a fun way to experiment sexually within the arms of someone you know and trust, but this scenario works better when it's a sexual treat, something enjoyed only every so often. This is for two main reasons. First, because the line between a FWB and an actual relationship can be thin and confusing. Add to the mix the fact that women can get attached to a repeat sexual partner and this lustful friendship might eventuate into a desire for something more. Second, when a FWB relationship emulates a real relationship, it can appear to take you off the market completely. If you have repeated sexual encounters with one person that bring you pleasure, combined with their friendship, intimacy and a connection (things most women crave from relationships), you might just take yourself off the market subconsciously without really realizing it. In other words, if your FWB situation is delivering many things you might need from a partner, your motivation to be out in the dating world could be low. Are you still going out, meeting other people and dating more men, or are you so content with your FWB scenario that you are no longer focused on your dating life? If you are still open to finding Mr. Right or Mr. Right Now, this special friendship could be getting in the way.

The Sleepover

I have gone to some crazy lengths to get men out of bed when they wanted to stay over. (Remember in Chapter 7 when I got a friend to call saying she was having dramas at a bar so I had a reason for a guy who wouldn't leave my apartment to skedaddle?) This is because I am aware of how sleepovers can change the dynamic of a relationship.

If you don't mind getting a little closer to someone you've hooked up with or are seeing, go ahead and sleep over; just be aware if you are ready for that. You are at your most vulnerable when you wake up in the morning: naked but for last night's makeup, bad breath and possibly needing to take a number two. To allow someone to see you in your vulnerability creates intimacy whether you like it or not.

It's always better to be the person who sleeps over rather than the host because it's far easier to get out of someone else's bed than to kick someone out of yours. If you do think there is a possible sleepover in sight, opt for a slightly larger handbag that can fit some morning essentials. My sleepover kit always includes: makeup wipes, a toothbrush, a small hairbrush, a phone charger and a little perfume.

No matter our motivations or intentions, there are times when alcohol and exhaustion simply can't stop a person from crashing between your sheets. If you do find yourself unable to get a man out of your bed, here are some suggestions to use in a pinch:

- You have a friend staying on your couch who is out at the moment but coming home later.
- You have to be up very early for a meeting/yoga class/ breakfast with a family member, so the alarm will be going off at 6 a.m. with a look that says, "I hope you don't mind."
- Ask him how he is getting home.
- Ask him if he wants you to call a taxi or Uber home for him.
- Don't turn the lights off, jump into bed or make the environment comfortable to sleep. Stay up and have a drink or put music on.
- Tell him you don't do sleepovers. It's your place and your bed and you have the right to dictate who sleeps in it. You might have invited him over for a good time but not sleepy time.

One way you might resolve this situation is to ask about his morning plans and tell him about your early morning meeting before you decide to go back to yours. That will set the precedent ahead of time that this is not going to turn into a sleepover.

If the sex is really good and you are having fun, you can always "cancel" that morning meeting.

Mini-Relationships

Thanks to the fact that we are having sex earlier in the dating scenario, or because sex is the way we start dating, mini-relationships can quickly develop in the SBD world. A mini-relationship is when two people jump into relationship-type behaviors without commitment or even knowing each other very well. They speed up the whole relationship process: having sex early, sleeping over straight away and simulating affections usually reserved for serious relationships. Perhaps mini-relationships happen because of a sense of urgency in the dating world today or as a way of quickly testing how a person might be if we did want to future date them. I also think mini-relationships can be an attempt to counteract the often superficial world of internet dating: more about having a need for intimacy rather than liking the person for who they really are.

My friend once saw a guy who, after only three dates, insisted on holding her hand down the street and ordering for her at restaurants, would say things like "This is so us" or, when she told him a funny story about her mom, said, "I can't wait to meet my hilarious mother-in-law." It was clear: they were in a mini relationship and, as the name implies, it had a short shelf life.

If you do find yourself in a mini-relationship, be aware of the motivation behind it (for both parties). Be honest with yourself, and if you find that you are participating because you're lonely, have low self-esteem or just want a boyfriend, it may be time for a man ban to press the reset button.

When Casual Sex Turns Serious

Casual is the way many relationships start off these days, as we do tend to take a more relaxed and spontaneous approach when it comes to dating, or at least it's become important we appear to be doing so. It gives us more freedom and more room for exploration, but as with all situations that begin casually, there is the risk that more will develop, as I mentioned in the sections on one-night stands, booty calls and FWB above.

If you want to take things from casual to a bit more formal and maybe out of the bedroom, you could suggest a nonsexual activity and see where it goes from there. If it's right, it might naturally progress into a relationship. Alternatively, you might realize that when you take this person out of the bedroom your so-called attraction isn't there and was merely a side effect of bonding during sex.

If the person you are having casual fun with was honest about wanting nothing more up front, then your honesty around developing feelings for them will likely not be taken well. This is also why, as a woman, you need to be careful what you say at the start of these casual scenarios, as you don't want to box yourself in. If you give a speech saying you're in it for fun and nothing more, you are limiting your alternatives and will make it harder to change your mind later if that happens to be the case. Even if you are almost certain you want something casual at the get-go, you need to be open to what life brings (and books like this that will make you thoughtfully question what you want). When you're starting out, be sure to say what you want, but add that you're open-minded if you want to keep your options open.

Have You DTR'ed Yet?

One of the difficulties when dating these days is when to have a conversation to define the relationship (DTR). If done too soon, trying to DTR with "So, what are we?" can be a sure-fire way to send a man running for the hills! If you are an SBD woman with options and a bit more mindfulness up your sleeve, hopefully you can relax for the first while and enjoy whatever the situation brings. The writing really should be on the wall if enough time is spent with someone, anyway. Look for a person's clues, key statements and behaviors when you are with them. Be careful to balance your potential negative analytical brain with your rational-sense vision. Try to see the situation for what it is. If you are still confused as to what the relationship is, then you can ask. Not in too serious a way that could make someone feel backed into a corner, but with a bit of playful banter and cheekiness to relieve the pressure of a potentially serious answer.

Moving On from *That* Guy

> *It serves me right for putting all my eggs in one bastard.*
> —Dorothy Parker

There is likely to be at least one guy who broke your heart. Even though you are now going about your life in the SBD world, there is probably still some attachment to this person and, quite possibly, it's blocking you from really moving forward and living your best life.

The memory of this person could be constantly rolling around in your head, making you feel a tad insane, or buried deeper beneath the surface, awakened only by triggers around the issues you experienced with him. You may feel there is unfinished business.

If it's revenge you are after—*walk away*! You do not want to be that person (think Glenn Close boiling a bunny in *Fatal Attraction*). It was after I'd been abruptly ditched by a guy I was head over heels for that I realized I was spending so much time thinking about what I could do to get him back that it kept me from moving on from him! I did get a little (probably harmless) revenge once when I had to put one ex's clothes in a bag and leave them for him to pick up. I might have put a copy of my book with a sticky note directing him to the section on Mr. Insecure. I couldn't help it. I also once bumped into a guy who hurt me very badly when I was on a date with a very handsome Englishman. The heartbreaker was on his own and looked put off seeing me enjoying myself. Being happy either on your own or possibly in the arms of another can be all the revenge you need, whether your ex witnesses it or not. For the most part, though, revenge isn't worth it. Go do yoga, ride a bike or take yourself on a weekend away until the feeling passes.

If you are after closure, the unfortunate truth is that you just might never get it. His perceptions of what happened are all but guaranteed *not* to give you the feelings of closure you are craving. You need to learn how to get closure from inside yourself.

If you find yourself talking about him to friends or discussing your heartache on constant repeat, stop! This is a surefire way to miss the life that is happening right in front of us. It was a light-bulb moment for me when I realized that thinking about this person was only keeping me attached to him and talking about him to my friends was only keeping him present in my mind.

Give yourself a big, swift kick in the bum and get realistic. The way I disconnect myself from the men who broke my heart is through smart self-talk and reasoning. I say things to myself like, "If he treated me like crap, why would I want to spend any more precious moments of my life thinking about him? This will only keep me mentally connected to him and the negativity he brought into my life." The time that you spend obsessing over the unanswered questions could be the time you spend moving on with your life, finding the next guy, taking up a hobby or achieving world peace, so have this simple conversation with yourself to jump-start healing.

Think about what triggers this person or your breakup pushed for you. Perhaps old abandonment issues or the feeling that you are never going to find true love, a husband or someone to take out the fucking garbage. If this is the case, then these are actually your own issues and there is nothing he can do or say to heal those old wounds. If this sounds familiar, it might be time to bring in a therapist to help you understand, digest and grow from those experiences.

Another great tip for getting over men who don't deserve us is to change their names in your phone to something that reminds you of why you are no longer with them. When they do call or text or when you get tempted to call or text them, seeing those words or names will revive your memory of the pain, distress or irritation they have caused in your life and how they did it. As time goes on, we might forget or distance ourselves from the pain they caused, so if we don't remember clearly why it all went wrong, we can be tempted into going back there. In my phone, I have Mr. Treats You Like Shit, Mr. Flaky and Mr. Never Can Return a Call. It's really hard to pick up the phone when Mr. Treats You Like Shit is calling.

It might take a while to stop thinking about him altogether, but take baby steps so that you aren't reminded of him at every turn. Change him on your FB from friend to acquaintance so he doesn't pop up in your daily feed. (I think it's great that he can still see how wonderfully you are doing, but don't go posting just to make him jealous. That is doing something for him and it will keep you attached.) Some may think that unfriending or "blocking" on social media may be immature, but if the level of hurt was severe enough (or if he's still trying to contact you), I believe this is an important step in protecting yourself and may be just what you need.

Last, you have a choice. If you want to be rid of him in your life, you can be. The choice is simple; you just need to make that choice over and over and over again whenever the situation arises. If you feel you are "trying" to be rid of him but not succeeding, it's time to take a good hard look at what the attachment to him or to the relationship is fulfilling in your life that you aren't ready to let go of. "Trying" in this case is simply an excuse to stay connected. It takes strength to really let go.

Don't Shit Where You Eat

Admittedly, it took a long time for this one to sink in for me. For a while there, I used the "Fuck it, I want it" approach with men across the board; I felt like I had missed out and was making up for lost time, sampling the buffet of different men and different dating and sex scenarios. I have never been romantically or sexually involved with a work colleague, but I have with classmates and neighbors. My advice? Proceed with caution.

I came home one night to find a neighbor having a party with lots of men hanging off his balcony. "Where's my invite?" I yelled to them sarcastically. I met my neighbor for the first time that night and we became friendly, swapping numbers in case I "needed anything." Soon after I left and jumped into bed, I got a text from that same neighbor: "Want some company up there?" I'd had a few drinks, was experimenting with newly single life for the first time since I was 16 and thought, *why not*? He was quite cute, after all. Things were all well and good until shortly after one of our nights of pleasure, he got back together with his recent girlfriend and she moved into our building! I don't know if she ever knew what happened, but every time I jumped in the lift or saw them around the building, the awkwardness was palpable. I didn't know if I should say hello or pretend I didn't know him. This is shitting where you eat.

There is an exception for every rule, so if there are strong feelings and a deep connection there and if you feel you might have a future together, then shitting where you eat could be worth the risk. If you are just having a bit of sexual fun, however, best not to do it with someone whom you will have to see each day by virtue of where you live or work—it only adds awkwardness and logistical complications to the already complicated situations in the SBD world.

He's Just Not That into You

Once upon a time, these simple words empowered us to move on from toxic situations. When he is calling, texting, making time to see you, bringing you food when you are sick or offering to help you out when you are in need, there is a good chance he's keen. If he's not calling, texting and so on, he's probably not keen. (Yes, there is the chance that he hasn't made a move because he's shy or thinks you are just not into him, but this is a far less likely scenario.) Here's the catch: he might be calling and texting every so often and *still* actually not be that into you. Mr. Just Not That into You can come disguised as someone else—Mr. Sending You Mixed Messages. Think of Mr. Sending You Mixed Messages as "Mr. He's Just Not That into You" extended a bit further: "Mr. He's Not into You But He's Just Horny and Sometimes Wants Sex or Attention."

It's also possible to find a Mr. *Kinda* Not That into You— he might like you enough to give you a little time of day, but it's ultimately for his benefit or with his agenda in mind. All men love having their ego fluffed and enjoy the company of a woman, so if they think you are an easy target, are into them or showing them kindness, then every so often they might send you the message that maybe they're into you. We have all been guilty of just trying someone on who is showing interest in us without the intention to reciprocate or enjoying attention from someone we are not really keen on.

A male friend of mine was not into this girl, but after her persistent calls and invitations, he went over to her place anyway. He ended up hooking up with her, only to remember midway why he didn't like her in the first place. I asked him why he went to her place and his response was, "I wanted to see what it would be like and was feeling a bit in the mood." This is how mixed messages are made. She thought all her Christmases had come at once; he was looking to test the waters, get off and find a quick way out. This type of confusing behavior actually has an official label—*intermittent reinforcement*—and it's a recipe to keep someone coming back for more (usually by taking advantage of their affection for you).

Intermittent reinforcement is a technique that is used to keep gamblers gambling. They might lose, lose and lose again, only to have a win and then lose some more. But that occasional and unpredicted win tells them that there is a chance for a larger future win, and that they should keep playing that machine.

This is the same thing that happens when a guy you like sends you mixed messages. Your desire to see him might be followed by rejection after rejection, a return call not answered or a text that takes forever to come back and then the occasional win—him! If he never returned your calls or texts, eventually you might get the message that he wasn't into you, but when he intermittently responds to you, teases you or even sends you an unsolicited message, it strengthens your belief that there is hope in sight.

To make matters worse, he might be pursuing you sexually, saying all the right things to get you into bed after not returning your calls and texts. You might think if he is in your bed and between your legs then he must be into you, but think again. It's simple: men love sex and are constantly in pursuit of it (like some women). If you are showing him some attention and affection and he knows he can get sex from you if he tries just a little, he just might use your eagerness to his advantage. Make sure you know the difference between when he's into you and when he's just into sex (and his own ego) and you're an easy target. Just like gambling, this is all about the numbers. Has the number of times he has replied, returned a call or caught up with you in person outweighed the times he hasn't? Be honest about that and you'll get your answer.

Be warned: it's a natural thing that we want what we can't have, so just when you work up the strength to leave Mr. Sending You Mixed Messages in your dust, there's a good chance he will come running. If he doesn't, then you really know he's not keen, but if he does, it sends yet another mixed message. Is he really into you, or has he come running back because you took yourself out of his picture? Staying unavailable for an extended period of time can be a good way to decipher between the two (as it will take his time and effort to continue reaching out over time), but it will never be a foolproof test of his true feelings.

If He's Playing Games

There are men out there who will use this same pattern (seeming keen one moment and cold the next) to deliberately pull you in and win you over. This marks a conscious attempt to play a game and its moves are calculated. They might be doing it because they suffer from low self-esteem and view "winning" you an accomplishment they need to feel good or they may just get enjoyment out of making a woman chase them. Don't feel the need to play games back. If you play games, you will only get games in return, and in game playing, someone has to lose.

How Does the SBD World Define Infidelity?

Infidelity. Cheating. Being unfaithful. When in an official relationship, these are pretty straightforward. In most SBD scenarios, however, they can be difficult to define—if they are defined at all. If you have just begun dating someone whom you are not exclusive with and are keeping it casual and haven't discussed whether you are seeing other people, you might still feel hurt or conflicted if you find out he is dating or sleeping with someone else. You're human. But you may not feel like you have the right to be hurt, having not established guidelines ahead of time. Be sure to define what your type of casual means in the context of whatever relationship you are having, or you could be in for a big miscommunication.

If you feel deceived by something that feels like cheating after wanting to keep things casual, this could be a sign that your feelings have become more serious. Before you become certain this is the case, make sure you aren't just feeling insecure yourself. Often we can experience jealousy when we are feeling less about ourselves because we become a bit fearful or anxious about the status of our relationships. If you have been getting a self-esteem boost from this casual situation and feel the risk of him going somewhere else, you may be jealous only because you fear losing what he brings to your life, not losing him as a person. Be honest with yourself about what you have been receiving from this casual situation and why the threat of losing it triggers you. If you don't need a man to boost your sense of self-worth and just wanted something casual, it should matter less whom else he is seeing and more how he treats you when he is with you.

In addition to asking yourself what cheating means in your SBD scenario, you also need to establish what you want to know about the other person's life. This might include whom else they are dating or it may not. That is a conversation I wish I'd had when dating one particular guy from my past. We both traveled a lot and I knew it was just casual, but there were genuine feelings involved. It was very new, so I didn't assume that it was monogamous, but I also hadn't considered he was dating other people. After returning from one trip, I called him and found out the next day was his birthday. Excitedly I said, "We need to celebrate, then! What are your plans?" He replied, "I have a date." I've never felt my jaw drop like that before. I wasn't as shocked that he was dating someone else as I was by how unabashedly open he was about it.

Trading Looks for Money

I am going to try not to offend anyone in this section, but I can't make any promises. I'm not talking about prostitution here, although you could argue this is nearly a form of it. Men of a certain financial situation, whether insecure or just enjoying the perks that come with money, know that they are able to get a woman who is good-looking (and I'm not telling you anything you don't already know). I think this is nearly the modern evolutionary model. Once upon a time, men were chosen for their ability to not only reproduce but to protect their family and to hunt and gather food to ensure the survival of their young. Maybe this is why many people view a strong body as one to be desired, as we still subconsciously associate strength with the ability to protect.

For men, this same reasoning was behind their choice in a partner—to ensure the survival of their young. Men chose women on their ability to reproduce. In modern society, many of those things we find attractive and sexy in the opposite sex subconsciously come from their association to effectively make a baby. These are the influences from our biological makeup and sometimes we feel as though these are innate and we have no control over them.

Today, it's not so much big muscles that ensure the survival of our young, but a big bank account. And it's not just survival women are after, but now also comfort and ease—which are part of the new definition of what it means to survive—and thrive—in the modern era. A man with money can be attractive to a woman regardless of his looks and physical stature, because he can provide her with stability, comfort and the enjoyable trimmings we value so much in today's society.

There is nothing wrong with finding a man's bank balance appealing—it can represent someone who is ambitious, driven and hard-working. It just shouldn't be your only criterion. If you are in the market to find a long-term relationship, then I can tell you from my time as a family mediator (assisting in the divorce process) that money does not equal happiness or relationship success—sometimes it just creates more problems. It's fine for a man to have money, but he also needs to have respect, love and consideration for you. You should value a man not by how much he earns but by how well he treats you, and not in the material sense—buying expensive gifts does not necessarily mean love and it is certainly not the recipe for lasting happiness.

Many women have been sucked into trading their looks for money and some even hunt it down. If you find yourself tempted toward this scenario, you need to keep your wits about you, be realistic and get your priorities straight. Know that your relationship might just be a tradeoff. Just as you are attracted to him for this particular financial quality, so may he be attracted to you for your physical beauty and possibly youth.

It's not rocket science: it's a tradeoff—and you both may be using each other. A superficial relationship is the price you pay for pursuing a superficial quality.

If you decide to engage in this type of relationship knowing its true dynamic, you will also want to consider what message it might send to others. This choice in partner might not only be intimidating for other men who feel as though, financially, they can't meet your expectations or wants, but they might also be turned off by your seemingly superficial motives. Even though you might see it as a harmless fling, it could have longer and lasting effects.

I have a friend who got sucked into the world of trading looks for money. I entertained it for a while, as I thought she was just experimenting with her dating life or it was just a stage she was going through. After they had been together for a year and it became apparent she really liked the perks that came with this life and man, I questioned her future plans. She told me that she would stay with him but still had her eye out for someone younger if he came along. They are now living together and it looks very serious, with no sign of a pending breakup or younger man in sight. The moral of the story is that when you are trading looks for cash, it's very possible that no one else will come along, as the message can seem clear: you are off the market!

Just as my friend (we aren't close anymore, but we check in from time to time) was willing to trade her man for a younger model, consider how easy it would be for a man using a woman for her youth and beauty to trade *her* in for a younger, more beautiful model. If your relationship isn't founded on true connection with an appreciation of the other person, you won't have the glue for longevity if that's what you're after. If you are only there for some short-term fun, ensure it's short term and understand the consequences of it, as you might be giving up your SBD status not for love but for the perks that this relationship brings.

Platonic Male Friends

Is a platonic male friend stopping you from meeting men? Platonic friends in your life can be wonderful, but you may want to monitor how much time you spend playing in their sandbox. Hanging with male friends in their territory can mean hearing the way they talk about other women—possibly in a degrading or sexual way—and that can impact you. Their chase for the perfect 10 might create toxic comparisons in your mind.

Another reality of a platonic friend is that (because men think about sex constantly) he's probably thought about having sex with you. You may have thought about having sex with him, too. You need to be wary of these mixed feelings, know how close you should get without giving mixed signals, know how to react if one of your platonic friends does make a move and be ready to let your platonic label be flexible if you do feel the friendship has something more in it. You might have been too quick to put him in that friend zone, unable or unwilling to see there may be something more in front of you.

There is always a way to test the waters if you have an inkling there is something more. Try to flirt a little more, be a bit more touchy, get a little closer while adding in some compliments: "You know there are not many men out there like you." You could even playfully ask, "Why did we never date?" Maybe it is a conversation that has just never been had, the contents of which will surprise you both.

As I've mentioned before, I don't like to encourage drinking and dating, but if you're not sure a platonic friend belongs in the friend zone, a few drinks just might be your answer. Just enough to put you both at ease so you can sniff out if there's chemistry between you that you haven't recognized. Who knows, you might just have a few drinks, feel sexual chemistry, hook up and continue on from the friend zone to friends with benefits (FWB). A few drinks might be the answer to cementing a more sexual type of friendship but not necessarily a date.

You should also be aware of the impact of a platonic husband—that one male friend you are really close to. Because he is able to provide what you need in a safe environment (besides the sex)—companionship, intimacy and someone to enjoy life with—he could easily keep you from putting yourself out there in the dating world.

This is very similar for gusbands, too—gay husbands. The gay world can be a safe and fun place for a straight woman to get companionship, but many also hide out there because dating can be scary and rejection can hurt. Use these friendships for enjoyment, and—as they are the same gender as those you are possibly dating—gusbands are a great source of information and advice, too.

In all of these cases, just remember to keep putting yourself out there in dating situations that can get you what you want in your dating, sex and love lives. A platonic husband and a gusband might feel satisfying in different ways, but they can't satisfy you in all the ways you deserve.

Chapter 9

What's Next

The most exciting, challenging and significant
relationship of all is the one you have with yourself.
—Carrie Bradshaw, *Sex and the City*

When I started on this SBD journey, I didn't realize how meaningful it was going to be in the larger picture of my life—I just thought I was having fun and experimenting with what it really meant to be free. Now, it's clear to me that *this*—feeling free to make decisions about your life based on what you want, not what you feel pressured to do—is what women need in order to find their individual happiness, and that we should, as a society, be more encouraging of freedom in sexual and romantic choices.

Being single is not about being sad, lonely, desperate or incomplete. In cultures around the world and in the not-so-distant past, women felt so much pressure to be in a relationship with a man—it was often considered the main focus of their life. They couldn't live this exciting, fun, surprising single life we get to live. Let's celebrate this lifestyle while we have it, not wait to appreciate it until we are reminiscing about it far in the future.

Listen to the women around you who are married or have been in long-term relationships. Some will be happy, but they will all have their fair share of complaints. Maybe they don't get enough time to themselves, especially if they have kids. Maybe they miss the days when they could be spontaneous, selfish and carefree. Enjoy this time in your life, because you might miss it when it's gone. If you spend all this time stressing over finding a man, when you do find him, you'll look back and say, "Oh, shit, I should have enjoyed that more!"

One of my friends who is married with two kids once told me that she missed having time to herself to read books—so I started reading more books. Appreciate the smaller things. A bed to yourself on the nights you want to hog the blankets, a bathroom where you can spill makeup everywhere and an entire closet to display your shoes (or, in my case, a linen cupboard as well). Sometimes it might be nice to have a partner around, but just as you practice mindful dating, practice mindfulness in general, too. Be positive and appreciate the life you have *right now* and the exciting SBD lifestyle you get to live that's teaching you so much (and giving you brilliant stories, to boot). Enjoy the journey; don't wish it away.

Aligning Your Thoughts and Actions

When you feel like moving on to a serious relationship, make sure your actions and thoughts match up. You might decide you have had enough of casual dates, hooking up and mini-relationships, but are you wanting to still play in the SBD world? Do you say one thing and do another? If you want to approach dating with a more serious and future mindset, then the actions of casually dating and hooking up will tell the people around you otherwise and turn away potential suitors whose intentions are more serious.

Your friends may be getting married and having kids, but these are not good enough reasons to give up on a life that's serving you the purpose you need at this time. Move on from the SBD world when *you* are ready, not because you feel you should (ditching that *should* curse).

Your actions might also give you an indication of what you need. If you find yourself unable to leave behind some casual dating behaviors, is it a clue that you need to stay SBD a little while longer? Or have you become a subconscious future dater? Have you stopped casually hooking up with men, floating around from date to date, and started to see requests that are not official dates as degrading? If so, you might be ready to move on and have not even become aware of it yet. Every so often, stop and reflect on what your actions and feelings toward dating are telling you about where you really are.

Marriage: One Path of Many

Many other dating books I have read made me feel as though finding a husband will solve all the problems in my life and that marriage is the ultimate goal. There are so many messages in our society that make women feel as though we are not enough, need other things to be fulfilled and that a ring on our finger makes us worthy and valuable. Even Beyoncé tells us to "put a ring on it." SBD is *definitely not* about changing yourself in order to get a husband; it's about focusing on and enjoying what you do have right now.

I have a lot of friends who are married. What I've learned from them is that they might have moved into a bigger house or had kids once they married, but they had already made the real commitment before they walked down any aisle. Doing so didn't solve all the dramas and stresses in their lives. They might not be worrying about a guy calling them back or whether a date went well, but they have a new set of worries, the negative consequences of which might be much more severe and life-changing. I'm not putting down marriage here, I'm just pointing out that a ring on your finger is not the ultimate answer (because I know that sometimes, in less empowered moments when you need to work on your esteem, it can feel that way). That's why I believe it's important to go through a period in life like the SBD years, when you can work out what you want and grow as a person, so you are ultimately able to enter a relationship from a healthy state of mind—not one looking for validation from a person or from "I do."

The next right step after an SBD life may be marriage for some and not for others. It depends on what you want and need deep down, and what you're ready for. Either way, I believe we should all continue going out in the world with that intention to improve ourselves and the mindset that we will meet great men. It's about continuing to enjoy your love and dating lives, whatever form that might take.

My Journey

A gentleman holds my hand. A man pulls
my hair. A soulmate will do both.
—Alessandra Torre

My motivation for writing this book was that I had been living the Single but Dating life for quite some time and didn't feel my relationship status had a place in society. I felt pitied for not being in an official relationship and that I wasn't being given the right advice for where I was.

It's what happened afterward that really surprised me. When I went into hibernation and put pen to paper and manicured finger to key, I really began to take my own advice. Everything I was writing, reflecting on and thinking about became ingrained in my Single but Dating brain. I went on a man ban, worked on my self-esteem and self-confidence and even froze my eggs. Eventually I even fell in love.

I'm not saying that if you follow everything in this book that love will automatically appear or that love is even the intention for everyone living this kind of life (some women just enjoy being SBD in general), but it was for me, and sharing my stories and advice was my way of saying goodbye to my SBD journey and hello to the next phase. The years I spent being Single but Dating were so vital—for me personally—to finding love.

In order to be a content person, I needed time to work out what was best for me. My SBD years got me to a point where I was able to appreciate something in front of me because it was what I wanted and knew would fulfill and enrich me, not because it was what anyone else was telling me I should want. I finally knew what type of relationship I wanted, what type of person I wanted to be with, how I wanted that person to make me feel and how I wanted to feel with them—and that's exactly what happened.

Dating has changed and continues to change more rapidly than ever before. We are a society that is inundated with options that make it very challenging to decipher what it is we truly want. Experimenting with and exploring the SBD lessons and ideas I've talked about in this book is our best defense to narrow down these options. If you know what you want and don't want because you've felt both, then you are in the best place to go and find it and to get rid of the blocks that get in the way.

I had to work on my strength both physically and mentally. Because dating is so hard, women need to have a bit of a thick skin. It's important that we still know how to be vulnerable under the right circumstances and the importance of feminine energy, but a low self-esteem is what drives so many women (including me, once upon a time) to make decisions around love and sex based on an unhealthy need for validation. If you've been guilty of this (I know I have!), don't have regrets about it. Nothing is ever a mistake as long as you can learn something from it.

You might not agree with everything I have said, but know that this book has been written out of love—from losing love to finding love within my own skin and eventually with someone else. I feel like I once lost myself, who I was and the life I imagined living. It took me years of hard work to discover not only how to truly love myself but how to make myself happy. It was only after that that I was able to really open my heart to another person. I continue even now to work on my self-esteem. I remind myself that if I love and respect myself enough, I won't put myself in situations where I will be disrespected or harmed or made to feel less than the powerful woman I am. I'm here to encourage you—and so is this book—to do the same.

I don't know the fate of my current relationship or what the future holds for me, but as I sit here writing this at this point in time, I am truly happy and fulfilled with someone else—something that has taken me years to be able to say and feel. I don't feel like I'm missing out on anything and I'm not fearful of the future. I'm also confident that if I can be this happy once and it doesn't happen to work out, I can be this happy again and I have the skills and tools to get there. The ongoing path to grow in love, relationships and great sex should never have an end point, so don't forget to enjoy it along the way.

Exercise—Key Messages

Everyone takes something different away from each piece of literature and each bit of advice. It's important for you to consider what the key messages are for you from this book that you will remember or implement in your life. In the space below, write five points that either resonated with you or that you will take on board for your dating journey.

1. _____

2. _____

3. —————————————————————————————

4. —————————————————————————————

5. —————————————————————————————

Exercise—New Goals

It's common that after reading through this advice and new information that some of your goals or intentions might have slightly altered or changed. If this is the case for you, in the space below, write three new or different goals or intentions you have after reading the book to take with you on your next steps in life.

1. —————————————————————————————

2. —————————————————————————————

3. —————————————————————————————

4. —————————————————————————————

5. —————————————————————————————

Acknowledgments

Thank you to all those without whom I could not have done this. Yes, the experiences throughout my SBD years taught me these lessons (many the hard way!), but you supported me through each of them and through the process of writing this book. Thank you.

To the boys and men I have dated, hooked up with, been in relationships with and fallen for, thank you for allowing me to experiment and experience the SBD world and discover what I want from life and love. Sometimes there were tears and heartache, but it all made me who I am today.

Thank you to those friends who supported me through the tears and heartache, as well as during my time of hibernation writing this book (and through my man ban).

Thank you to my therapist, who helped me build my self-confidence, assisted me as I worked through my obstacles and helped me to be the best version of myself. Thank you to my gym for pushing me physically and making me strong so I could push myself mentally and professionally.

Thank you to my manager, Simone Landes. Before we met, I may not have been the type of girl who was looking for the perfect man, but I was looking for the perfect manager—and then I found you. Your advice, wisdom and support have kept me going and motivated. I might have already lived the life of an SBD girl, but you were the one to help me get it to paper!

To Christine Bronstein and Mickey Nelson from Nothing But The Truth, thank you for giving this Aussie girl a go and publishing my SBD ideas. In a world that seemed so big and scary, you have made things so easy, warm and welcoming.

Thank you to all the experts and friends I have interviewed for this book—your advice, knowledge and opinions have been invaluable to me.

Thank you to my amazing family. I am so fortunate to have such a wonderful support system of people who not only teach me lessons in life and love but who are there for me when I need it the most. You are my world and my world would be nothing without you.

And to a special person who showed me I could really love again and for being in love with me, thank you. I started to doubt that feeling this way was possible, but then you found your mermaid in a pool.

And, finally, to all of you who have picked up this book, whether single or friends with someone who is—thank you for supporting my work and believing in yourselves enough to know you deserve happiness *right now*, wherever you are on your journey. I wish you all the best and only hope you find happiness in your life.